Past Masters
General Editor Keith Thomas

Proust

Derwent May is a novelist and critic, and is the Literary and Arts Editor of the *Sunday Telegraph*. His novels include *The Laughter in Djakarta* (1973) and *A Revenger's Comedy* (1979), and he is also the author of *Hannah Arendt* (1986) in the Penguin series, *Lives of Modern Women*.

Past Masters

AQUINAS Anthony Kenny
ARISTOTLE Jonathan Barnes
AUGUSTINE Henry Chadwick
BACH Denis Arnold
FRANCIS BACON Anthony Quinton
BAYLE Elisabeth Labrousse
BERGSON Leszek Kolakowski
BERKELEY J. O. Urmson
THE BUDDHA Michael Carrithers
BURKE C. B. Macpherson
CARLYLE A. L. Le Quesne
CERVANTES P. E. Russell
CHAUCER George Kane
CLAUSEWITZ Michael Howard
COBBETT Raymond Williams
COLERIDGE Richard Holmes
CONFUCIUS Raymond Dawson
DANTE George Holmes
DARWIN Jonathan Howard
DIDEROT Peter France
GEORGE ELIOT Rosemary Ashton
ENGELS Terrell Carver
GALILEO Stillman Drake
GIBBON J. W. Burrow
GOETHE T. J. Reed
HEGEL Peter Singer
HOMER Jasper Griffin

HUME A. J. Ayer
JESUS Humphrey Carpenter
KANT Roger Scruton
LAMARCK L. J. Jordanova
LEIBNIZ G. MacDonald Ross
LOCKE John Dunn
MACHIAVELLI Quentin Skinner
MARX Peter Singer
MENDEL Vitezslav Orel
MILL William Thomas
MONTAIGNE Peter Burke
THOMAS MORE Anthony Kenny
WILLIAM MORRIS Peter Stansky
MUHAMMAD Michael Cook
NEWMAN Owen Chadwick
PASCAL Alban Krailsheimer
PETRARCH Nicholas Mann
PLATO R. M. Hare
PROUST Derwent May
RUSKIN George P. Landow
SHAKESPEARE Germaine Greer
ADAM SMITH D. D. Raphael
SPINOZA Roger Scruton
TOLSTOY Henry Gifford
VICO Peter Burke
VIRGIL Jasper Griffin
WYCLIF Anthony Kenny

Forthcoming

ARNOLD Stefan Collini
BENTHAM John Dinwiddy
BLAKE Marilyn Butler
JOSEPH BUTLER R. G. Frey
COPERNICUS Owen Gingerich
DESCARTES Tom Sorell
DISRAELI John Vincent
DURKHEIM Frank Parkin
ERASMUS James McConica
GODWIN Alan Ryan
HERZEN Aileen Kelly
HOBBES Richard Tuck
JEFFERSON Jack P. Greene
JOHNSON Pat Rogers

KIERKEGAARD Patrick Gardiner
LEONARDO E. H. Gombrich
LINNAEUS W. T. Stearn
MALTHUS Donald Winch
MONTESQUIEU Judith Shklar
NEWTON P. M. Rattansi
ROUSSEAU Robert Wokler
RUSSELL John G. Slater
SOCRATES Bernard Williams
TOCQUEVILLE Larry Siedentop
WITTGENSTEIN Anthony Grayling
MARY WOLLSTONECRAFT
    William St Clair
and others

Derwent May

Proust

Oxford   New York

OXFORD UNIVERSITY PRESS

Oxford University Press, Walton Street, Oxford OX2 6DP

Oxford New York Toronto
Delhi Bombay Calcutta Madras Karachi
Petaling Jaya Singapore Hong Kong Tokyo
Nairobi Dar es Salaam Cape Town
Melbourne Auckland

and associated companies in
Beirut Berlin Ibadan Nicosia

Oxford is a trade mark of Oxford University Press

First published 1983 as an Oxford University Press paperback
and simultaneously in a hardback edition
Paperback reprinted 1986

British Library Cataloguing in Publication Data
May, Derwent
Proust.—(Past masters)
1. Proust, Marcel
I. Title   II. Series
843'.912   PQ2631.R63
ISBN 0–19–287612–0
ISBN 0–19–287611–2 Pbk

May, Derwent, 1930–
Proust.
Bibliography: p.
Includes index.
1. Proust, Marcel, 1871–1922—Criticism and interpretation.
I. Title.   II. Series.
PQ2631.R63Z78257   1983   843'.912   82–14492
ISBN 0–19–287612–0
ISBN 0–19–287611–2 (pbk.)

Printed in Great Britain by
The Guernsey Press Co. Ltd.
Guernsey, Channel Islands

Contents

Note on references

References after quotations are given in the following form: (III P100, K95). The roman numeral refers to the volume number, which is the same in both the French and the English texts cited. 'P100' means page 100 of the edition of *A la recherche du temps perdu* in the *Bibliothèque de la Pléiade*. 'K95' means page 95 of Terence Kilmartin's revision of the translation, *Remembrance of Things Past*, by C. K. Scott Moncrieff. Fuller details of these editions are given in the suggestions for further reading at the end of the book.

Quotations from the translation are included by kind permission of Chatto & Windus Ltd and Random House, Inc.

I would like to thank Mr D. J. Enright, Mr P. N. Furbank, Mr Keith Thomas and Mrs Jacqueline Simms for their helpful comments on the manuscript version of this book.

D. M.

1 Proust and his novel

Most readers know a little about Proust. He drank a spoonful of tea with some crumbs of a French cake in it (a *madeleine*, in fact, a cake that looks as if it has been moulded in a scallop shell) — and suddenly he remembered the whole of his childhood, because his aunt used to give him a piece of *madeleine* dipped in lime tea when he visited her as a child on Sunday mornings. After that experience — so the common impression runs — he spent many years working in a cork-lined room putting all his memories down. His three-thousand-page autobiographical novel was translated by an Englishman, C. K. Scott Moncrieff, who is almost as much to be admired as Proust. But — and this thought is not always so clearly formulated — 'it doesn't sound as if it has much to do with life as we have to live it'.

There are some grains of truth in this impression. But in all essentials it is wrong. In the first place, it confuses two quite different people. It is Marcel, the narrator of *A la recherche du temps perdu* (literally, 'In search of lost time'), who puts the famous spoon to his lips; and Marcel is not the same as Proust, though Proust was of course himself called Marcel. (Henceforth in this book, 'Marcel' will mean the narrator, and 'Proust' will mean the author.) Proust drew deeply on his own experience for the portrait of Marcel; nevertheless, Marcel is always seen as a character, the object of scrutiny and sometimes of irony. We are dealing with a created world, with all the control and flexibility that implies, not just a remembered one. Proust did indeed have an experience like Marcel's over the tea; but — with the characteristic difference that there is between all the events in Proust's life and their equivalents in the novel — it was a piece of moistened toast that he tasted early in 1909, and it was his childhood visits to his grandfather that he then recalled.

There is an even more unfortunate error in the common impression of Proust. It is the suggestion that Proust's novel is mainly about the lyrical childhood reminiscences of a sensitive recluse. *A la recherche* contains that element. But what people who have not read it fail so often to realise is that it is a great comic novel. It is also a dazzling study of French character and society, and an intricate work of history. And it was written by a man who lived as much in the *haut monde* as he did in his imagination.

From 1910, when he was thirty-nine, till 1919, three years before his death, Proust certainly spent most of his time in an enormous bedroom in his flat on the Boulevard Haussman in Paris – a bedroom which had panels of cork nailed to the walls and ceiling, long blue curtains belonging to his great-uncle that were always drawn, and a perpetual smell of fumigating smoke in the room to help his asthma. Here, lying in bed, in many layers of sweaters, he wrote his novel. But very often, late in the evening, he would get up and dress, and go out to parties with the writers and aristocrats who had become his friends in earlier years. He was famous for his witty conversation; he was generally the last to go home from the parties or receptions; and when he got back at two or three in the morning, he would go on talking, sitting on the end of his bed describing the evening's experiences to his servant, a young woman called Céleste Albaret, whom he admired so much that he eventually put her into his novel under her own name. 'He was a Persian poet in a porter's lodge,' said the French critic, Maurice Barrès, implying a great deal, but not least his tendency to do things like sit on the bed and talk to Céleste.

Another fine critic of Proust, the German writer Walter Benjamin, is, I think, absolutely right when he says that Proust was inspired by 'a frenzied quest for happiness'. Proust was dismayed when he first heard that '*A la recherche*' – 'in search of' – was being translated into English as '*Remembrance of*'. He had been a seeker since he was very young; he was not just a rememberer.

Proust's early life

His grandfather kept a shop in the small town of Illiers, not far from Chartres; his father, born in 1834, became a distinguished doctor in Paris and married a cultured Jewess, Jeanne Weil, the daughter of a wealthy stockbroker. Proust himself would always have plenty to live on. He was born in the Paris suburb of Auteuil on 10 July 1871. In his early childhood, Illiers, rather than Paris, was where he was happiest, and the exquisite childhood memories in the novel all refer to Illiers, which takes the name 'Combray'. He went through the usual sequence of lycée (the Lycée Condorcet), military service, and the Sorbonne, where he took a degree in philosophy. As a young man he quickly saw where the charm of life lay for him: it was in Paris upper-class society, still dominated by the pre-Napoleonic nobility, who may have been rich and haughty, but who were welcoming to artists and clever men who knew how to please them. Proust soon made his way in this world, starting with the upper middle-class salons of such women as Mme Strauss, who was the mother of a schoolfriend and widow of the composer Bizet. Before long he was the acquaintance, and sometimes the friend, of many of the members of the highest stratum of French society at the end of the nineteenth century: 'the Faubourg'. This meant 'the Faubourg Saint-Germain', a district of traditional aristocratic houses on the Left Bank of the Seine – though by the 1880s it had become the name of a set of people rather than of the *quartier* where they lived, since many had moved to the newly fashionable districts of the Right Bank.

Proust has sometimes been sneered at as a snob for his cultivation of this milieu. It seems a feeble-minded sneer, whether one considers the intensity of imaginative delight that he took in the contemplation of this world, or the depth and subtlety of his criticisms of it. Nevertheless he was an outsider in various ways, and well aware of it. Apart from his comparatively modest family background, he was an artist (he had been publishing in literary magazines since he was twenty-one); he was half-Jewish; and, as he early came to realise, he was homosexual.

In 1897 the Dreyfus Affair burst upon France. Three years earlier, a Jewish army captain called Alfred Dreyfus had been found guilty of passing secrets to Germany, and exiled to Devil's Island. Now it suddenly appeared that he was innocent of the crime, and that the army were not only suppressing evidence in his favour, but actually forging new evidence against him. Proust knew where his loyalties lay. He was one of the writers and intellectuals most energetic in getting names for a petition to the government, demanding that the case should be opened again — a campaign that did lead, in due course, to Dreyfus being rehabilitated. But Paris society was seriously split by the case. A majority of the upper class supported the army out of blind patriotism, and found common ground with 'anti-Dreyfusards' from the middle classes. However there was a substantial minority in the Faubourg who rallied to what was seen to be the cause of reason and truth. One of the most remarkable aspects of *A la recherche* as a historical novel is its portrayal of this rift, and of the quite different way in which Paris society regrouped itself after the Dreyfus Affair.

Throughout these years of what might seem rather frivolous social life — years, too, in which he had a number of love-affairs, the earlier ones heterosexual, the later ones homosexual, and all of them fairly unhappy — Proust was writing. In 1896, when he was twenty-five, he published his first book, a collection of sketches and short stories called *Les plaisirs et les jours*. By now he had also begun a long novel, which he abandoned after several years, and which was only published in 1952, under the title *Jean Santeuil*. Both in the stories and in this first novel, there is much material that was later transformed into scenes in *A la recherche*. But *Jean Santeuil* was evidently, for Proust, too simply and straightforwardly an autobiographical story: it had not got the vast overall design, and the consequent depth of significance in its detail, that he was to achieve in the story of Marcel.

He became an enthusiastic reader of Ruskin, and published translations of *The Bible of Amiens* and *Sesame and Lilies*. In 1908 he brought out a series of brilliant parodies of nineteenth-century French writers, in which his own gift for observing and creating nuances of style was dramatically shown, and which were perhaps an essential step in his search for his own distinctive voice, discovery through a necessary rejection. (They were first published in book form in 1919, in the volume *Pastiches et Mélanges*.) Next, Proust turned to a long, hostile essay on the critic Sainte-Beuve. He wanted to distinguish his own view of literature from Sainte-Beuve's, which put the emphasis on the writer, not the book; however, this work slowly grew from being an essay into a series of what looked like episodes in a novel. These scenes, again, would appear in a new form in *A la recherche*. (But, like *Jean Santeuil*, this work, under the title *Contre Sainte-Beuve*, was not published until many years after Proust's death, in 1954.)

It was in 1909 – perhaps, in part, through the incident of the tea-flavoured toast – that the theme and form of his great novel seem finally to have become clear to Proust. In 1910, as we have seen, the cork panels went up in his room. From now onwards till his death, he was to find his happiness above all in working on his book.

'Lost time'

The search for lost time, as the title correctly says, was to be the key to it. But this does not just mean the rediscovery of childhood – an impression you might receive, incidentally, from reading George D. Painter's otherwise remarkable biography of Proust. *A la recherche* is a much more complex odyssey than that, in which the 'lost time' being sought comes to include the long years of rich experience during which Marcel is obscurely searching for it. Marcel's final discovery, well after the 1914–18 war, is – like Proust's in 1909 – the discovery of how to write his book. But this discovery, important though it is, is far from being the overwhelming point of the book. Rather, it is what enables us to have the book, with all its other wealth of interest. There would be less point in Marcel's remembering, if there was not so much to remember.

This enormous wealth of interest, and the exuberance with which it is created and conveyed to us, is the first thing to stress in a study of Proust's novel. From one point of view, *A la recherche* is like a tremendous piece of gossip – like the eighteenth-century memoirs of the Duc de Saint-Simon, which Marcel's grandmother is always quoting. Quite late in the story, Marcel is coming home with his mother from Venice when they learn about two unexpected marriages among his aristocratic friends. Back home in Paris, in their dining-room, this leads the two of them to start reminiscing. 'Thus there proceeded,' says Marcel,

> one of those long chats in which the wisdom not of nations but of families, taking hold of some event, a death, a betrothal, an inheritance, a bankruptcy, and slipping it under the magnifying glass of memory, brings it into high relief ... It is the wisdom inspired by the Muse ... who has gathered up everything that the more exalted Muses of philosophy and art have rejected, everything that is not founded upon truth, everything that is merely contingent, but that reveals other laws as well: the Muse of History. (III P675, K692–3)

That Muse, though Marcel gives her a place below the highest, inspires a great deal of what is most arresting in his narrative.

For an intimation of the other truths – the truths 'of philosophy and art' – that lie beneath this surface vividness, we can turn to a different scene, the one in which Marcel is first invited to the home of the Princesse de Guermantes, for a late-night party. In the Princess's garden there is an eighteenth-century fountain, supposedly designed by a real painter, Hubert Robert. Proust (or Marcel) describes it:

> It could be seen from a distance, slender, motionless, rigid, set apart in a clearing surrounded by fine trees, several of which were as old as itself, only the lighter fall of its pale and quivering plume stirring in the breeze ... But from a closer view one realised that it was a constantly changing stream of water ... its thousand separate bursts succeeding only from afar in giving the impression of a single thrust. This was in reality as often interrupted as the scattering of the fall, whereas from a distance it had appeared to me dense, inflexible, unbroken ... (II P656, K680)

We can find many analogies to Proust's novel in this fountain, as no doubt he intended us to. The illusion it gives of a single, unbroken thrust is just the kind of illusion that gossip and history give, a seductive illusion that Marcel himself sometimes accepts, and allows us to share with him. But look closer, and one sees not a single jet, but a 'thousand separate bursts'. In just the same way, Marcel discovers and shows us the manifold separateness that in fact constitutes human experience. People are separate from each other: they do not understand each other, they survive on fantasies about each other in which the truth hardly finds a lodging. The broadly coherent impression that an outsider gets of a relationship has nothing in common with what the people involved in the relationship are going through. There is separateness within the individual's own experience: one impression, one emotion, has no connection with another. These are some of the truths that Proust's 'Muse of philosophy' would like to teach us.

Part of Marcel's quest is to try to counter this agonising separateness in some way – and here the fountain may take on another symbolic meaning, besides that of human illusion. It can also symbolise art, the means by which, Marcel comes to believe, separateness can be triumphantly, if with great difficulty, overcome. We must not forget that an artist made the fountain, as we must not forget anything else that we read in Proust as we go along: for everything in fact is related to everything else in the book.

The passages I quoted may themselves be seen as similar to the fountain. The reader will have noticed several sets of dots where sections have been omitted. By making these omissions, I have given these passages a clearer 'single thrust'. In the full text, that thrust is as much interrupted as the rise and fall of the fountain.

We may find an analogy for this in another part of the novel where the tone is quite different. A witty passage describes the way in which one of its most sympathetic great ladies, the dowager Marquise de Cambremer, writes her letters. Well-bred people at the time observed the 'rule of the three adjectives': always use three adjectives when describing things. 'What was peculiar to her,' we are told, 'was that the sequence of the three epithets assumed in Mme de Cambremer's letters the aspect not of a progression but of a diminuendo.' When she invites Marcel to dinner she says that she will be 'delighted – happy – pleased' to see him. Marcel speculates that 'her desire to be amiable outran the fertility of her imagination' (II P945–6, K977–8). It is hard to believe any desire could have outrun the fertility of Proust's imagination. But he too, in a disconcerting way, will let a thought run on to a second or third formulation, each one making connections that take him far away from the point that, on a simple view, one might have expected him to be making.

To find an explanation of this, we may look at a description he gives of Chopin's piano music. It happens to be in another episode concerning Mme de Cambremer. She had learned to play Chopin as a girl, and still cherishes

> those long sinuous phrases ... so free, so flexible, so tactile, which begin by reaching out and exploring far outside and away from the direction in which they started, far beyond the point which one might have expected their notes to reach, and which divert themselves in those fantastic bypaths only to return more deliberately – with a more premeditated reprise, with more precision, as on a crystal bowl that reverberates to the point of exquisite agony – to clutch at one's heart (I P331, K361).

Like Chopin as described in that sentence, Proust only goes off in an unexpected direction in order to pave the way for coming back, often much later, to some essential theme that will swell out to fullness.

The whole design of the novel illustrates this. It must have taken extraordinary confidence on Proust's part to begin his great portrait of Marcel with a long story about a man who is as old as Marcel's father – Charles Swann, the wealthy man of fashion whose love-affair with the cocotte, Odette, takes up most of the first part of the novel, *Du côté de chez Swann* ('Swann's Way'). But the description of the Chopin phrase gives us the clue to Proust's intention here. In Marcel's very different love-affair with Albertine, which dominates the middle part of the novel, the 'notes' of *Du côté de chez Swann* return exactly as Proust says – 'with a more premeditated reprise, with more precision', so that the novel 'reverberates to the point of exquisite agony'. This is one of the many triumphs over separateness in the book.

The story of the novel

We shall conclude this chapter with a brief outline of the story of the novel. It should already be clear that this is not a novel whose essence lies in its plot. But there are countless dramatic incidents, unexpected changes of direction in people's lives, revelations of further depths in a character. And though Marcel's mind is forever moving away from the immediate event he is describing to memories and comparisons, drawn both from life and from art, there is a broad progression of events through the years. In particular, the narrative dwells on seven great parties, at all of which many threads in the story closely intertwine.

Du côté de chez Swann ('Swann's Way')

Combray ('Overture' and 'Combray'): Here we meet Marcel as a boy, staying with his mother and father at his great-aunt's house in Combray. Other important figures in the family life are his devoted grandmother, and the ebullient, sharp-tongued servant, Françoise. Charles Swann is a middle-aged neighbour who likes to call on the family sometimes in the evenings when he is at his house at Tansonville. None of the family realises what a brilliant social life Swann leads in Paris. It is when Swann is visiting them that Marcel goes through the agony of waiting in bed for his mother's good-night kiss. There are two walks which the family go on when they are in Combray — one past Swann's house, 'Swann's way', and one in the other direction past the ancestral home of the noble Guermantes family, 'the Guermantes way'.

Un amour de Swann ('Swann in Love'): Here the story goes back a number of years to describe Swann's life as a younger man in Paris, especially his love-affair with Odette de Crécy. Odette has in the past lived on men (and perhaps still does) but she is not what we would now call a prostitute. She is kept by the lover to whom she is currently giving her favours, but she is expected to be faithful to him. Swann and Odette have a genuine love-affair (though he gives her plenty of money) and he frequently goes with her to the house of a rich, ambitious woman, Mme Verdurin. Mme Verdurin at this time has scarcely any connections with 'the Faubourg' (where Swann himself is completely at home), but she has high social pretensions as a patron of artists and intellectuals. She is the source of a great deal of the comedy in the novel, but, as we shall see, she achieves the highest possible social standing by the end of the book.

Swann goes through tortures of jealousy over Odette, who is soon unfaithful to him, and the first great party takes place at the time when he is resigning himself to the loss of her love. He goes to the house of the Marquise de Saint-Euverte, where we meet the dominating figure of the Faubourg: Oriane, the future Duchesse de Guermantes, who is a close friend of Swann's. She still has only the lesser title of Princesse des Laumes (she and her husband become the Duke and Duchess when her father-in-law dies) but she already feels that she is being distinctly gracious and condescending to come to the salon of such a minor aristocrat as Mme de Saint-Euverte.

Swann finally leaves Odette, though later in the novel we find that he does, after all, marry her; mainly, we suppose, because she has borne him a daughter, Gilberte. We are also led to understand that Marcel has learned about Swann's history partly from Swann himself, when Marcel is older, and partly from the talk of other people.

Noms de pays: le nom ('Place-Names: The Name'): Here we see Marcel as a slightly older boy in Paris. He is falling in love with Swann's daughter, Gilberte, meeting her sometimes when he is out in the gardens of the Champs-Elysées with Françoise. He is also dreaming of Venice and Florence, and of a seaside town in Normandy called Balbec, where he has been promised a holiday.

A l'ombre des jeunes filles en fleurs ('Within a Budding Grove')

Autour de Mme Swann ('Madame Swann at Home'): Marcel's love for Gilberte increases, but receives little response, and he discovers the pains of jealousy and of separation. However, he is also discovering the pleasures of the theatre, and his literary ambitions are being encouraged — if rather faintly — by his father's friend and superior in government service, the ambassador M. de Norpois. His friend Bloch, also an aspirant writer, introduces him to a brothel. He often goes to Mme Swann's house, in the end to see her as much as to see Gilberte, and it is there that he meets the great writer, Bergotte.

Noms de pays: le pays ('Place-Names: The Place): Marcel at last goes to Balbec for a long summer holiday, with his grandmother and Françoise, staying in the Grand Hotel facing the beach. The landscape and sea scenes intoxicate him in different ways from those he has anticipated. He meets a wider social circle: an elderly marquise who is a member of the Guermantes family, Mme de Villeparisis; her great-nephew, the lively and kindly Robert de Saint-Loup, at this time a young army officer; a mysterious baron, likewise one of the Guermantes, M. de Charlus; an impressionist painter, Elstir; and a girl called Albertine, who is the most striking of a noisy band of girl cyclists who are constantly on the front at Balbec. Albertine spends a night in the Grand Hotel, and invites Marcel to visit her in her bedroom; but when he tries to kiss her she rings the bell.

Le côté de Guermantes ('The Guermantes Way')

Marcel and his family have moved to another district of Paris, and have a flat in part of the mansion belonging to the Duchesse de Guermantes. Marcel's boyhood visions of her give way to first acquaintance with the reality of her personality; he falls in love with her from a distance. He becomes obsessed by the sight he has of her at the Opéra in the box of her cousin by marriage, the Princesse de Guermantes. He goes to Doncières to stay with Saint-Loup at the barracks, partly to try to persuade Robert to introduce him to the Duchess, who is Robert's aunt. He gets invited to the second great party of the novel, a *matinée* (or tea party) given by Mme de Villeparisis, whom he met at Balbec. Here he meets again the Baron de Charlus, who takes a deep but − to Marcel − puzzling interest in him. He is also introduced at last to the Duchesse de Guermantes. At this party he finds that the Dreyfus Affair is beginning to send its reverberations through Paris society.

Marcel's grandmother has a stroke when she is out with him in the Champs-Elysées and soon afterwards she dies. Albertine visits Marcel in Paris; he has a feeling, apparently correct, that she is more sexually experienced than she was in Balbec, and they begin a rather cool liaison. Marcel's love for the Duchess fades away; but she invites him to a dinner party, which is the third great party in the book, full of revelations about the behaviour of the upper stratum of the Faubourg. Marcel goes to visit the Baron de Charlus, who assaults him with violent criticism for not showing proper appreciation of his kindness. Marcel pays another evening visit to the Duke and Duchess of Guermantes and (in one of the most brilliant scenes of the book) sees how completely the demands of social life overrule all other considerations for them.

Sodome et Gomorrhe ('Cities of the Plain')

Marcel, from a hiding-place, accidentally sees an encounter between the Baron de Charlus and Jupien, a tailor who has his shop in the courtyard of the Guermantes house. Through this he realises that the Baron is a homosexual — an explanation, in part at least, of his behaviour towards Marcel. Marcel goes to a late-night reception at the home of the Princesse de Guermantes — this is the fourth great social event of the book (it is on this occasion that Marcel observes the fountain described above). His impressions of this milieu are further enriched and confirmed. The Dreyfus Affair has also gone a long way by now in its work of creating unexpected divisions in the *haut monde*.

Marcel becomes more preoccupied with Albertine, but also begins to suffer more from his realisation of 'the intermittencies of the heart'. Mme Verdurin's salon, and Odette's salon, both begin to rise in social importance. Marcel goes to Balbec again, largely in hopes of meeting a lascivious maidservant who he believes has gone there with the family she works for. But the belated realisation of his grandmother's death overwhelms him, in this hotel which he first visited with her; and his entire being seems to him to be disrupted.

Albertine is also in Balbec, and he starts seeing her again, after all. But he now begins to suspect that she is having Lesbian love-affairs. In pace with the growth of that suspicion, his obsession with her also grows. The Verdurins are staying at La

Raspelière, a country house near Balbec, and he and Albertine often visit them. Charlus falls in love with a young violinist, Morel, who is doing his military service at Doncières; Morel is a habitué of the Verdurin 'Wednesday evenings', and takes Charlus along with him, to the fifth of the book's big parties. Charlus and Morel are now like Swann and Odette used to be, when they went to the Verdurin salon in its earlier years. But the first big clash between Mme Verdurin and the Faubourg is brewing. Marcel goes for drives around Balbec with Albertine in a chauffeur-driven car; he decides he will break with her, but at that moment learns that she knows a pair of Lesbian lovers whom he spied on once as a boy at Combray – the daughter of a composer called Vinteuil, and her friend. All his fears about her infidelity to him return with redoubled force, and he decides he must marry her so that she shall not go out of his sight again.

La prisonnière ('The Captive')

Marcel is living in the family flat in Paris with Albertine; his parents are away. He is happiest when she is lying asleep, and he is lying awake listening to the morning street sounds. When she goes out he is always worrying about where she might have gone. In this volume of the book, his ideas about music and literature develop considerably. The climax of the volume is the sixth great party, which also takes place at the Verdurins', now back in Paris in a new house. All day Marcel has been fearing that Albertine is meeting Lesbian friends, on an outing she has made to the Trocadéro; eventually he sends Françoise to bring her back. He dissuades her from going to the Verdurins' party in the evening, because he suspects the Vinteuil girl and her friend may be there; but while she remains at home, he goes there secretly himself. He witnesses the climax of the war that has developed between Mme Verdurin and the Baron over Morel. Mme Verdurin is gravely snubbed by the aristocratic visitors whom the Baron has brought; but she succeeds in getting Morel to leave the Baron. There is a performance at the Verdurins' of a work by Vinteuil, who was also the composer of a sonata of which a phrase used to haunt Swann at the Verdurins' years before when he was first in love with Odette. This work revives

Marcel's flagging faith in art. When Marcel goes home, he has a quarrel with Albertine; and soon afterwards she leaves him. Françoise, who has always hated Albertine, is happy.

La fugitive ('The Fugitive')

Marcel tries to get Albertine to come back; but the 'intermittencies' of his heart continue. Then he learns that she has been killed in a riding accident. It takes him a long time to recover from his love for her, strange love though it was. He visits Venice with his mother, and there discovers both fresh happiness and a deeper sense of desolation. Saint-Loup marries Gilberte; but it appears that he has now become − perhaps always has been − homosexual and is in love with Morel. Another unexpected marriage − between Jupien's niece, an uneducated girl who has been adopted by Charlus, and a young aristocrat − startles Paris society even more.

Le temps retrouvé ('Time Regained')

Gilberte is living again in Tansonville, nominally with Robert; but he is not often there. Marcel visits her as a guest. They walk out together, and he learns what he could never have imagined in his boyhood: that 'Swann's way' links up with 'the Guermantes way'. The symbolism here need not be stressed.

Marcel has to go away to a sanatorium because of his health. He returns to Paris during the war, in 1916, and finds many changes. Mme Verdurin's salon, particularly, has gone from strength to strength. On a later visit, he finds that Charlus's homosexuality has become much more obvious and desperate; the Baron goes to a male brothel for flagellation. Saint-Loup is killed at the front.

Many years later, after the war, Marcel comes back to Paris again. He goes to the seventh and last of the great parties, once again at the Princesse de Guermantes − but the now Princesse de Guermantes is the former Mme Verdurin. Completing the union of the two 'ways', the Duc de Guermantes has become the lover of Odette, Swann having died long ago. Marcel finds that all these old friends have become extremely aged, and almost unrecognisable. But it is now that he begins to see what his book must be about, and how he can write it: it will be about the passage of time, and the conquest of time. It is, we suppose, the book we have just been reading.

2 Society and snobbery

One of the neighbours of Marcel's family at Combray is a M. Legrandin, an engineer from Paris with a rather fanciful, literary way of speaking. He is quite liked by the family, but one day they see him after church with a lady who owns a big country house, and he gives the impression that he does not know them. Another Sunday Marcel watches his deep bow when he is introduced to the wife of another large landed proprietor: he springs sharply backwards as he comes out of it and, says Marcel, 'this rapid straightening-up caused a sort of tense, muscular wave to ripple over Legrandin's rump, which I had not supposed to be so fleshy' (I P124, K135). Legrandin has a sister married to a minor nobleman living near Balbec, and later, when Marcel's holiday there is being planned, his father asks Legrandin politely if he knows anyone in the neighbourhood of Balbec, in case anything should happen to Marcel's grandmother while they are there. Legrandin airily avoids the question, saying 'There as elsewhere, I know everyone and I know no one' (I P131, K143). But when Marcel asks him if he is acquainted with the Guermantes, he declares he is far too independent to want to know such people and fiercely attacks snobbery as the vilest sin, the sin against the Holy Ghost. Even the young Marcel can see at once that it is the sorrow of his life that he does not know the Guermantes.

In this way, through Legrandin, Marcel gets both an enhanced sense of the glamour of the Guermantes, and, though he does not know it yet, an illustration of precisely the kind of snobbery that he will eventually find dominating the lives of the Guermantes as well. There are two sides to it: the construction for oneself of a social position, by letting the world know one maintains it, and by doing everything to reinforce the claim; and the erection of a defence for oneself against the feeling that one is not, in fact, part of a milieu one would like to belong to. Legrandin practises both these things — though he scarcely knows he is practising either. And he is fairly unsuccessful in both of them: he doesn't convince anybody of his social position, neither those people he believes superior to him nor those he believes inferior; and he suffers a good deal of distress.

The Guermantes family

Later, when Marcel knows the ways of the Faubourg, he is able to say plainly: 'Almost all society people are so insignificant that they are judged only by their success' (II P648, K672). But in the Guermantes family he does at least encounter the wholly successful. Of course, their position in the Faubourg owes something to their wealth and to their titles. But there are other families who equal them in these respects. Their pre-eminence is due above all to the style and confidence with which they assert it. It has nothing to do with 'good manners', with being gentlemanly or ladylike – though these are weapons in their armoury that they can employ with brilliance and ease when they want to. The Prince de Guermantes declares his status on the very steps of his house, when he is visited by the Princesse de Parme. He comes down to greet the Princess at the foot of the steps, but he gives no indication of having seen her friend and companion, Mme d'Hunolstein, standing by her. Only when all three of them reach the top of the steps does he suddenly seem to notice the other lady, when he greets her as affably as he has greeted the Princess. But he has shown that he does not have to come down to welcome her at the foot of the steps.

The Duc de Guermantes, the Prince's cousin, always greets Marcel's father with courtesy when he meets him in the courtyard, often straightening his coat-collar for him. But even in this gesture he is indicating that he comes of a line of royal body-servants. He strokes Marcel's father's hand – but manages to convey as he does so 'that he did not begrudge him the privilege of contact with the ducal flesh' (II P33, K28). He is always sure of the desirability of his presence, and of the rightness of his ideas. He calls on Marcel's family in order to offer his sympathies when Marcel's grandmother is on the point of death, and makes plain his displeasure with Marcel's mother when he sees that she is too distracted to listen to his speeches; he decides eventually that she must be slightly mad. When Marcel shyly tells him that he had an article the previous morning in *Le Figaro*, the Duke roundly declares that Marcel must be mistaken — he saw no such article when he read the paper.

But it is the Duchess, Oriane, who is the outstanding example that Proust gives us of this skilled social domination. She is on very bad personal terms with the Duke, but in public they co-operate faultlessly. If commoners are for any reason invited to her house, she talks charmingly to them. To a young girl, for instance, she will wax enthusiastic over the girl's father's great qualities, but her tone will be indistinguishable from what it would have been if she were recommending him for a gardener's job. In the Faubourg she holds the supreme position. She manages this by the greatest care in the issuing and accepting of invitations, making herself very exclusive; and also by a daring and a wit that put her in a class of her own among the great ladies of her social sphere. The young Comtesse Molé, calling on the Duchess, finds she is without visiting cards and leaves instead a large envelope addressed to herself that she has in her pocket. The Duchess is both somewhat offended and not to be outdone in originality. Swann has just brought her a gigantic, blown-up photograph of some coins he has been studying, and she orders a footman to take the enormous envelope containing it, on which the photographer has written 'La Duchesse de Guermantes', round to Mme Molé's.

Her success is attested by the number of gifted men who have, effectively, given up their careers to be part of her circle. Some, like a certain diplomat and doctor, have suffered from the jealousy of their professional colleagues, or the feeling that they are less reliable because of these fashionable and reactionary connections. Others have simply found the charm of being one of the Guermantes circle sapping their interest in their legal or parliamentary career, and slowly stopped bothering about it.

The Baron de Charlus, who is the Duke's brother, is the most vicious defender of his and his family's position. He tries to see that no one is invited to the Princesse de Guermantes's receptions without his authority (and is the more annoyed to find Marcel there). One of the Princess's guests at her late-night party is that Mme de Saint-Euverte at whose house we first met the Duchess, when she was still Princesse des Laumes. Mme de Saint-Euverte is giving a reception on the next day, and has come partly to 'hold an eleventh-hour review of the troops who were on the morrow to perform such brilliant manoeuvres at her garden-party', as well as to issue a few more strategic invitations (I P669, K694). But in the Baron's eyes she is socially worthless. When Marcel clumsily asks him if he is going to her reception, he says, within earshot of her, 'This impertinent young man has just asked me whether I was going to Mme de Saint-Euverte's, in other words, I suppose, whether I was suffering from diarrhoea ... They tell me that the indefatigable old street-walker gives "garden-parties". Myself, I should describe them as "invitations to explore the sewers"' (II P700–1, K726).

The proof that social standing comes simply from an interaction between what people believe themselves to be and what other people believe them to be, is that Mme de Saint-Euverte, after she has heard these words, is still flattered when she bumps against the Baron a moment later, by the chance it gives her of speaking to him; and she says 'Oh! I beg your pardon, Monsieur de Charlus, I hope I did not hurt you' – 'as though she were kneeling before her lord and master'.

All the Guermantes are particularly sarcastic about the new nobility created by Napoleon. Charlus says, for instance, that when someone spoke to him of the Princesse d'Iéna, he supposed she must be 'some poor wanton' who slept under the Iéna bridge on the Seine, and had 'picturesquely assumed the title' (II P564, K586). In fact, at the barracks at Doncières we meet an officer who is a Napoleonic prince, the Prince de Borodino, and we find that he has his own confident way of dealing with the social situation in his regiment. Among the officers junior to him there are both aristocrats from the Faubourg and commoners; but he looks down on them all 'from the height of his Imperial grandeur' (II P130, K130), and invites the plebeians whom he likes to dinner, while keeping the aristocrats in their places lest they should show improper pretensions. Yet, Proust observes, the Prince de Borodino, conscious that he has a title that still preserves its meaning, is always distinctly patronising to his guests, while his junior, Saint-Loup, an unselfconscious member of a caste which has lost all its power but none of its sense of its own distinction, is genuinely friendly to anybody he likes, no matter what his origins — his friendship with Marcel being a good example of this.

Charles Swann

The character in whose life the complex and arbitrary nature of social standing is most clearly mirrored is, however, Charles Swann. At the beginning of the novel, Marcel's family, particularly the old ladies still living in Combray, still see him as the son of the stockbroker who was a friend of Marcel's grandfather; also, they know he is married to a woman of dubious morals, whom they will not receive; so when Swann comes to the house, Marcel's great-aunt feels he ought to regard it as a privilege, and bring them a present of raspberries or peaches from his garden. They have no idea that he may have a letter from the Prince of Wales in his pocket, or that the Duchesse de Guermantes may be anxiously awaiting his return to Paris for a party she is giving.

Yet when he marries Odette, who is as unwelcome in the Faubourg salons for social reasons as she is among Marcel's family for moral ones, Swann falls effortlessly into an acceptance of her set of social values. If some senior civil servant comes to dinner, for instance, he and Odette are both equally pleased; and if a boring woman comes, Swann will go out of his way to find attractive qualities in her. In this latter respect, in fact, he is drawing on a style he has acquired from the Duchess, though in very different circumstances. When the Duchess invites tedious Grand Dukes or Princes of the Blood, she insists on finding them agreeable — or how could she justify their presence there? She is not going to admit her true, snobbish reasons. Swann actually behaves with equal naturalness at home with his wife or in the Duchess's drawing-room, sincerely expressing the social judgements appropriate to each place.

The Duchess is genuinely fond of Swann (or at least, Marcel later remarks, has the illusion that she is when she is listening to his conversation). But when he is ill, and knows he has not many months to live, he sees himself become a victim of the standards of the Faubourg. It is the occasion on which he has brought Oriane the photograph of the coins. The Duke and Duchess have an engagement for dinner which has already been threatened by another dying man, the Duke's cousin Osmond, who is likely to 'croak' ('*claquer*'), as the Duke puts it, that very night. The Duke has been making prodigious efforts not to learn of Osmond's death, should it occur, since that would make it impossible for him and Oriane to go out. He has sent a footman to enquire at Osmond's and to come back quickly while he is still alive, so that he will not need to enquire again.

When Swann comes, Oriane says she would like him to accompany them to Italy the following year. Swann says it is impossible — and reveals that he will be dead in three or four months. But now the coach is at the door, and the Duke and Duchess must go. 'I don't know why I'm telling you this,' says Swann, with instinctive politeness; 'whatever I do, I mustn't make you late.' The Duke hurries his wife out, telling Swann he doesn't believe a word he's saying. Then, just as they are getting into the coach, he notices she is wearing black shoes with a red dress. He makes her get out and go back to change them. The Duke and Duchess have time to ensure that they look right for their party; they have no time — their social obligations being what they are — to listen to a dying friend (II P595, K618).

One regret of Swann's is that the Duchess will not only not receive Odette, but will not receive his daughter Gilberte either. It is even said that when he married Odette, one of his main reasons was his longing that, in time, Gilberte would be received by her. It is only after his death that his wish is granted — when he can no longer provide Oriane with 'the exquisite sensation that she was resisting him' (III P577, K589). However, the change only produces a turn for the worse in Swann's posthumous standing. He becomes a victim, now, of Gilberte's snobbery. Gilberte does not scorn the family who have always snubbed her; on the contrary, they assume even greater importance in her eyes because of it, and she gladly accepts their invitation. She tries to euphemise her father's name — Jewish in origin — by saying 'Svann' instead of 'Souann', the English way in which he pronounced it (though then she realises it sounds German, which is even worse). Her mother has married again and she adopts the surname of her stepfather. Finally she begins to hint that Swann might not even have been her father. People tactfully cease to mention him when she is present – that is to say, on the principal occasions on which they might have mentioned him. And so the delightful and gentle Swann passes out of social sight, when he had expected that it was precisely through his daughter that his name would live.

Changes in the Faubourg

When Marcel first discovers the Faubourg, and this passionate social game that it plays, it seems to him that the rules, which he slowly deciphers, are something fixed for ever. In a certain sense this is true: newcomers, new generations, are going to be driven by similar passions. But events of another order do make their impact on this fragile world that is so largely a product of shared fantasies, fantasies that the skilful project and the weak accept. 'Social manifestations,' says Proust, 'though vastly less important than political crises and artistic movements, are nevertheless an echo of them, distant, disjointed, uncertain, changeable, blurred' (II P742, K769).

The Dreyfus Affair is one such outside influence. The Baron de Charlus is mainly concerned with the way the Faubourg is being adulterated by it:

> 'All this Dreyfus business,' went on the Baron, still clasping me by the arm, 'has only one drawback. It destroys society ... by the influx of Mr and Mrs Beasts and Beastlies and Fitz Beastlies [*de messieurs et de dames du Chameau, de la Chamellerie, de la Chamellière*], whom I find even in the houses of my own cousins, because they belong to the Patriotic League, the Anti-Jewish League, or some such league, as if a political opinion entitled one to a social qualification.' (II P290, K300).

Other members of his family treat the Affair more seriously, however. The young Saint-Loup, who is an enthusiastic if fanciful socialist when Marcel first meets him, is naturally a Dreyfusard; and even the Prince and Princesse de Guermantes, for all their intense interest in their own social position, come to believe in Dreyfus's innocence. As for the Duc de Guermantes, he is converted to being a Dreyfusard by three charming ladies he meets at a spa. (Proust never lets us suppose that we can predict anything in human behaviour.) However, such aristocratic renegades do not in practice do much to upset the harmony of their own society. The real beneficiary of the Dreyfus Affair in the novel is Mme Verdurin.

As we saw earlier, Mme Verdurin, though an extremely rich woman, has very little contact with the Faubourg. Her defence is to regard aristocrats in general as 'bores'. 'Bores', she often repeats, are what she will never have in her salon. It is essentially a literary and artistic salon, with a painter, an academician, a learned doctor of medicine (all of them, incidentally, excellent comic portraits) as its 'regulars' from the start. Mme Verdurin is herself an ardent Wagnerian, who has worked up an elaborate performance to express her suffering and her aesthetic rapture when she listens to Wagner. But she quickly sees the possibilities for her in the Dreyfus Affair. Though at one time fiercely anti-Semitic, she now makes her salon a home for the Dreyfusards, thus drawing many new and distinguished people into her net. Later, when the Russian Ballet comes to Paris with Bakst and Nijinsky, Mme Verdurin becomes the sponsor of 'these new great men', and appears 'wearing on her head an immense, quivering aigrette that was new to the women of Paris and that they all sought to copy' (II P743, K770).

Mme Verdurin's great clash with the Faubourg comes through the Baron. He makes himself a regular at her gatherings, for the sake of Morel, who likes giving concerts there. On the whole he conceals his contempt for her, and contents himself with private mirth at her pretensions and her ignorance of 'real' society. But he overreaches himself when he arranges a musical evening for her, inviting many of his connections from the Faubourg and excluding most of her own friends. Mme Verdurin is thoroughly humiliated: the guests pour into her drawing-room, greet the Baron, and totally ignore her, or even make insulting remarks about her in her hearing. She has her revenge: she manages to persuade the volatile Morel that he must break with the Baron, for fear of social disgrace and even, possibly, of criminal charges being brought against him. The Baron's collapse after Morel's desertion is the beginning of his personal and social decline, whereas Mme Verdurin goes on from strength to strength.

The rise of Odette Swann's salon is also helped by the Dreyfus Case, in a different way. She is violently nationalistic and anti-Dreyfusard – and she wins a great deal of approval from the Faubourg for this, since her husband's Jewish origins might have discouraged her from coming out so boldly. And there are two spectacular social ascents witnessed by Marcel. He has seen a young girl, Rachel, in a brothel. He is not much attracted to her, but he never forgets the casualness with which she prostitutes herself, saying to the brothel-keeper, 'Don't forget I'm free tomorrow, if you want someone send round for me'. He is astounded to find, a little later, that his new friend Saint-Loup is desperately in love with her, heaps her with money and presents, and has set her on the road to being an actress, her real ambition. She achieves great fame on the stage, and we last see her, many years later, as a friend of Oriane, Duchesse de Guermantes. One of her first public performances had been a recitation at Oriane's, and it had been a total failure. But just as the Duchess's long refusal to receive Gilberte merely enhanced the Duchess's prestige in her eyes, so Rachel's failure had left her for ever wanting to be a member of the Duchess's world.

The other transformation is that of Jupien's niece, who worked in his shop. But this is a brief and poignant episode. Morel at one time wants to marry her, then impulsively rejects her. However the Baron de Charlus, in his perverse way, adopts her, and even manages to acquire a grand title for her. A young aristocrat marries her – the son of the Marquise de Cambremer (who, to complicate the social story still further, is the sister of Legrandin who lives near Balbec). But Jupien's niece dies of typhoid a few days after the wedding. Still, she has become a member of the highest aristocracy. Thus, says Proust, the death of a simple little seamstress plunges all the princely families of Europe into mourning.

With the rise of new powers in Paris society there goes, in the end, the fall of the old ones. As we have seen, Mme Verdurin's final triumph is to become Princesse de Guermantes herself, by marriage to the old Prince (Proust does not say so, but perhaps her championing of Dreyfus brings her this last reward, if we remember that the Prince once became attracted to the cause). At the reception she gives, in the last part of the book, all the Faubourg are there as her guests. It is now something like fifty years since Swann went to the Verdurin evenings with Odette. But Odette is still alive, looking like a 'sterilised rose' (III P950, K993), and – another capitulation of the Faubourg – the Duc de Guermantes, a very old man himself, is her lover. With the new generation, the Duchess has largely lost the position she once held. Opinions and styles have changed; moreover, in her self-confident way she has started cultivating actresses and other Bohemians, and this has further reduced her standing. Only the very old dowagers still regard her with awe.

The most tragic figure in this scene, even allowing for the arrogance and cruelty of his earlier way of life, is the Baron de Charlus. Marcel sees him in the street outside the Princess's house. His silver hair and beard make him look like King Lear. But his eyes have lost their brilliance, and all his moral pride has gone. As Marcel watches, old Mme de Saint-Euverte, whom Charlus once so despised, passes in a victoria:

> And immediately, with infinite laboriousness ... M. de Charlus lifted his hat, bowed, and greeted Mme de Saint-Euverte as respectfully as if she had been the Queen of France or as if he had been a small child coming timidly in obedience to his mother's command to say 'How do you do?' to a grown-up person. For a child, but without a child's pride, was what he had once more become. (III P860, K891–2)

Marcel and society

Marcel first becomes aware of the Guermantes family as a boy in Combray, and from the start he fantasises about them. 'You're always talking about Mme de Guermantes,' says his mother (I P174, K190). He is haunted by the thought of the long continuity of their family line. He pictures the real Duke and Duchess as tapestry figures, like that of the Comtesse de Guermantes in the 'Coronation of Esther' which hung in the church, or as stained-glass figures in iridescent colours, like that of Gilbert the Bad in the church, or as being like the Guermantes ancestress, Geneviève de Brabant, whose image he would send wandering over his curtains or ceiling with his magic lantern.

One day the Duchess comes to Combray for a wedding, and he is amazed to see she is an ordinary woman, with a red face and a pimple. 'So that's Mme de Guermantes – that's all she is!' he thinks. But a moment later, something very important happens: suddenly, as he realises that 'she had a real existence independent of myself', he feels she is acquiring an even greater power over his imagination, which had been 'paralysed for a moment' by contact with a reality so different from what he had expected. Just as he experiences this sensation, she looks at him, and he 'cries out within himself': 'How lovely she is! What true nobility! It is indeed a proud Guermantes, the descendant of Geneviève de Brabant, that I have before me!' (I P175–7, K191–3).

The realisation of the independent existence of the outside world always has some such effect on Marcel. It alarms and upsets him, as his earlier fantasy loses control; and then it stimulates him to go out and make a fresh conquest of what he has just perceived. This further conquest will itself often be most important as a conquest of the mind or imagination, even if it entails a real social or sexual conquest. Then he will be at peace again – but bored; and once more he will need the stimulus of some disturbing and independent object of interest. In subsequent chapters we shall see how this powerful trait in Marcel's personality connects with other aspects of his thoughts and feelings, and comes to form the basis of his whole concept of art.

A few years later, when he finds he is living in the same building as the Duchess, Marcel falls in love with her; he has not been introduced to her, but he hangs around for hours in the street, hoping she will pass and notice him. As we have seen, he quite quickly manages to make her acquaintance and that of her milieu – starting with the lucky chance that his grandmother knows Mme de Villeparisis; next, meeting Mme de Villeparisis's great-nephew, Robert, who takes a great liking to him and much admires his intellect and his conversation; then finally, because he is both Robert's friend and an interesting and charming young man, gaining entrée to the rest of the Faubourg. But of course, when he gets to know the Guermantes family and all its friends, he quickly realises what frail and foolish people most of them are. Once he crosses the magic threshold of the Duchess's house, its spell quickly begins to fade. His love for the Duchess also soon disappears, though with his incorrigible tendency to hopeful fantasy, he turns his thoughts for a while to the Princesse de Guermantes – until he makes her acquaintance, too. Proust, in fact, writes about the whole of this episode in Marcel's life with a degree of irony (and does it, very brilliantly, through Marcel's own narrative): he shows us Marcel's gaffes in the ducal drawing-rooms, and his even more absurd social triumph when he makes exactly the right, distant bow to the Duc de Guermantes – which inevitably reminds us of Legrandin's bow, Marcel's first glimpse of the follies of snobbery.

We are going to see so much that is strange and distinctive in Marcel's attitude to life that it is as well to stress here the amount of sheer ordinary, natural interest that he takes in this milieu, which is, after all, a rather remarkable one. He is never fiercely critical of it – comedy and pathos, rather, are what he sees in the Faubourg's ardent but limited passions, and what Proust's novel superbly conveys to us. Its fascination for Marcel is a recurrent one, too: in him, the process of unease, agitation, desire, conquest and boredom can go on repeating itself with the same people. (And very much the more so, as we shall find, when he is in love.)

Yet many years later, when he looks back on this period of his life, Marcel feels that he never experienced pleasure when he was in the company of the Guermantes, only when he was alone afterwards, distinguishing their characteristics in his mind. He learned a great deal from being in their company – but what he mainly learned was that their life was not for him. He continues to value certain qualities that he found in the Faubourg. He still

admires the ease and confidence displayed by its best represen-
tatives – as we have seen, what he thinks the Baron has lost at
the end of his life is a definite virtue, his 'moral pride'. Marcel
particularly remembers the courtesy and kindliness of Saint-
Loup, which would stop at nothing to serve a friend, and which
came from the same aristocratic confidence – there was an
occasion in a café when he thought Marcel was feeling cold, and
he ran along the ledge behind the occupied banquettes by the
wall, in order to bring him a cloak he had borrowed from the
Prince de Foix.

As for the Duchess, Marcel still recalls the charm of her un-
shakeable style, as when she had Swann's giant envelope
delivered to the Comtesse Molé. But with her it is something else
that he particularly appreciates – a way of speaking she has, a
harsh, ancient, rural savour in the sounds, combined with a
purity of vocabulary 'that might have been used by an old
French writer'. It is almost like listening to an old song, while
seeing, 'imprisoned in the perpetual afternoon of her eyes, a sky
of the Ile-de-France or Champagne spread itself, grey-blue,
oblique' (II P495, K514).

So in his conclusions about the Duchess, Marcel reverts to the
kind of myth-making he used to engage in before he met her,
creating a more subtle continuity between her and her family's
past, that takes into account things he has now observed in her,
but moving away from her real personality again, in the end, to
a comforting idea of her. And at the very end of the book – as a
man of about fifty, who is just about to begin a great, subtle
novel evoking the infinite variety of French social life – we find
the same tendency still present in him. When he looks at Mme
Verdurin, now Princesse de Guermantes, he is at first miserable
to think that she has nothing in common with the Princesse de
Guermantes who once cast her spell on him. Then, suddenly, he
finds solace: for ever and ever, he thinks,

> there would come, sweeping on, a flood of new Princesses de
> Guermantes – or rather, centuries old, replaced from age to
> age by a series of different women, of different actresses
> playing the same part and then each in her turn sinking from

sight beneath the unvarying and immemorial placidity of the name, one single Princesse de Guermantes, ignorant of death and indifferent to all that changes and wounds our mortal hearts. (III P956, K999)

The boy who dreamed of the Guermantes has acquired a man's experience; but he is still there in Marcel's mind.

3 The sufferings of love

Swann: the foreshadower of Marcel

At the book's first great party at Mme de Saint-Euverte's, as
Swann goes up the monumental staircase lined with liveried at-
tendants, he thinks how much happier he would be going up the
dark, smelly stairs to an attic where a certain little dressmaker
lives — a friend of Odette's, with whom he could have sat and
talked, and so brought himself a bit nearer to the side of
Odette's life that was always a mystery to him. He remembers
how at night, on those stairs, an empty, unwashed milk-can is
set out on every door-mat.

Milk is always associated with peace of mind in *A la
recherche*, and peace of mind is what Proust's lovers seek,
though they hardly ever find it. When he first meets Odette,
Swann has got over his younger passions, and it is a kind of calm
that Odette brings him when she starts paying him afternoon
visits, fashionably-dressed but shy and affectionate. He is not
even very attracted to her sexually — he is regularly seeing a
plump little seamstress at the time — but he starts going to Mme
Verdurin's evenings with her. It is only one night when he
arrives late at Mme Verdurin's and Odette has already left that
he finds how much he needs her. He seeks her everywhere in the
Paris night, in all the restaurants and cafés. Women approach
him in the streets, but he brushes anxiously past 'these dim
forms, as though among the phantoms of the dead, in the
realms of darkness, he had been searching for a lost Eurydice' (I
P230, K252). Suddenly he collides with her, and he takes her into
his carriage. That night they become lovers.

Proust manages marvellously to convey in these pages how a
woman who, as Swann later concludes, was never his 'type' at
all, becomes so important to him. But Swann's happiness is not
very long-lived. He begins to suspect that she has other lovers,
and soon his preoccupation is less with seeing her than with

knowing she is not with someone else. He himself reflects 'how small a thing the actual charm of Odette was in comparison with the fearsome terror which extended it like a cloudy halo all around her, the immense anguish of not knowing at every hour of the day and night what she had been doing, of not possessing her wholly, always and everywhere!' (I P346, K376). But she invariably denies that she is unfaithful, and Swann is never completely certain that she is. He learns the art of reassuring himself: he starts remembering the moments when she is good to him and joining them together, abolishing the intervals between them, casting 'as in molten gold the image of an Odette compact of kindness and tranquillity'. In fact, we are led to believe that she is constantly deceiving him. He does not know how to cope with the situation. He makes speeches to her about her frivolity, but what she sees clearly is that his speeches mean that he loves her — so she does not bother about what he is actually saying.

The reader will already have noticed a marked similarity between Swann's behaviour with Odette, and Marcel's need to control and assimilate any elusive object of interest, if necessary by means of fantasy. At one point, in fact, Swann wonders if he himself put into Odette all the things he loved in her — if they weren't really there at all. This makes us think immediately of a passage conspicuously placed on the fourth page of the novel, where Marcel alludes to the experience of a man having an orgasm in his dream. He says that the woman visualised in such a dream seems to be offering pleasure, but is in fact conceived by the dreamer from his own pleasure. This remark, as we shall see, might be made about much of Marcel's experience in his waking life. Real women may provide the initial stimulus for his love; but after that it is less what they do than what he thinks about them that brings his happiness. In this respect, especially, Swann's affair with Odette foreshadows Marcel's experience.

The main difference between them, as Marcel himself observes in due course, is in what makes them suffer, rather than what makes them happy. 'Swann was incapable of inventing his sufferings — they came from without,' Marcel says (I P283, K309). He means that Swann's sufferings, at least, were caused by something real — Odette's real infidelity. Marcel's sufferings, on the other hand, come 'from within' as much as his joys do; he is as fertile in imagining infidelity and desertion by women as he is in imagining possession of them.

Certainly both Marcel and Swann, in the love-affairs of theirs that we are shown, want total possession of their women, at least in their mind. They want the woman to have no more of an independent life than the woman in the dream has. We suppose, says Marcel much later, that love has for its object a being who can be laid down in front of us, enclosed in a body. 'Alas!' he continues, 'it is the extension of that being to all the points in space and time that it has occupied and will occupy' (III P100, K95). Only when we feel that we can touch every point of that extended being can we find contentment: that is why happiness in love is ultimately impossible. Or so Marcel comes in the end to believe, a process we must now examine.

The first women in Marcel's life

As a child, Marcel goes through agonies waiting for his mother's good-night kiss when his parents have evening visitors. There is one night when he particularly angers his mother by the fuss he makes, but his father unexpectedly intervenes and suggests that, just for once, she might spend the night in Marcel's room. Then she forgets her anger, and smilingly offers to read to him. He feels guilty, but finds both misery and guilt being swept away as she reads, putting all her own 'natural tenderness' and 'lavish sweetness' into the words of George Sand. 'My aching heart was soothed,' Marcel says. 'I let myself be borne upon the current of this gentle night...' (I P42–3, K45–6).

It is a beautiful scene, but also a prophetic one. Marcel himself is aware, as a man, of the similarities this night has with his other, rare nights of contented love. They too will be nights when he feels secure in the possession of a woman, and the recipient of all her tenderness. But even as a child he knows that such a night can never be repeated with his mother.

He finds a similar 'assuagement of his anguish' with his grandmother, on his first visit to Balbec as an older boy. He feels lost and ill on his first night in the hotel. This is not the Balbec he imagined – the external world is declaring its stubborn independence again. Everything around him seems hostile

– the clock in his room, the bookcases even: he has 'no world, no room, no body now that was not menaced by the enemies thronging round me' (I P667, K717). But his grandmother soothes him; she herself seems to find an 'exquisite pleasure' in giving him 'a moment of immobility and rest' for his weary limbs, and helps him undress. On subsequent mornings, when he is unwell, as soon as he knocks on the wall of her room next door, she comes in with milk for him.

When Marcel is young, he takes what is in many ways quite a normal, 'healthy' interest in girls. While still quite a child, he is struck by a glimpse he has of Gilberte in Swann's park at Tansonville; later, in Paris, falling in love with her, he plays with her whenever he can in the gardens of the Champs Elysées, and successfully schemes to get himself invited to her parents' house. But some of his more unusual tendencies are also already apparent. His imagination reaching out to embrace all around Gilberte, he seems to fall in love as much with the place she is in as with her as a person. One of the most famous passages in the novel describes how, already thinking about Gilberte, he sees her through a hawthorn hedge he has just been delighting in. The path he is on throbs with the fragrance of hawthorn blossom; in particular, one pink thorn-bush embedded in the hedge among its white flowers makes him think of 'a young girl in festal attire' (I P140, K153). At that moment he sees Gilberte, with her fair, reddish hair and bright black eyes. She is always associated with the hawthorn hedge after that, in his memory. But he transforms her into a picture of his own from this first moment, too. He remembers her eyes as being of the 'vivid azure' that seems to match the colours of the scene, even though he knows their real colour. He says, in fact, that he loves their imagined blue the more because of their brilliant blackness. He is provoked, we might say, into making things more harmonious for himself the more they insist on their discordant individuality.

We also see in this first scene with Gilberte his prudishness and lack of realism about women, which he never really loses. She makes a rude gesture that he thinks is meant to be an insult. Only years later, when they are both middle-aged, does he learn from Gilberte that it was her way of making some kind of childish sexual suggestion. (Or at least so she says – for never can you completely trust anything anyone says in *A la recherche*.)

Gilberte never loves Marcel, however, and his passion for her dies painfully. His friend Bloch awakens him to the idea that all women have sexual desires, and the idea excites Marcel greatly; but when he goes to a brothel with Bloch, he is disappointed, and only goes back, characteristically, to talk sometimes.

We get another strong impression of what stirs his feelings when he sees a girl from the train on his way to Balbec for the first time. Already exalted by the scarlet sunrise and hilly landscape, he notices a tall girl approaching the little station at which the train has stopped. She immediately 'embodies the quintessence of the place' for him (I P655, K705). Her face comes nearer, and it seems like the sunrise itself. She looks at him – and he wants to be attached to her and this new life for ever. The train moves off, and he resigns himself to losing her, though he goes on day-dreaming about returning to live near the station. What the girl was carrying as she came up to the train was a jar of milk.

Marcel and Albertine

In his love-affair with Albertine, which dominates the middle part of *A la recherche*, we find the features of all these early relationships returning. Marcel first sees her as one of a band of bicycling girls on the front at Balbec. He immediately and for ever afterwards associates the girls with their setting; they are rose-sprigs whose principal charm was that they were silhouetted against the sea, or they are a flock of gulls, or they are the perpetually moving waves of the sea themselves. He only slowly distinguishes Albertine as an individual: the girl in the polo-cap, and perhaps the most striking of them. Even then, like Swann with Odette at first, he does not find her especially attractive sexually; some of the other girls excite him more.

He cannot make the girls out. To begin with, their raffish ways lead him to think they are the rather juvenile mistresses of professional cyclists. But he meets Albertine at the studio of the painter Elstir, and discovers that she is the niece of some prosperous business people in Paris – friends, indeed, of Odette – and is considered a perfectly respectable young woman. However her social origins and standing remain throughout the novel very unclear. Having met her, he starts going out for cycle rides with the girls. He is still attracted to all of them indiscriminately, but is particularly curious about Albertine.

The moment when he feels himself to be falling in love with her is very expressive of him. He and 'the band' and some other young men and girls are playing a game of 'ferret' (*'furet'*), in which a ring on a cord is passed deftly round a circle of players who are holding the cord, and the person in the middle of the circle has to guess who has the ring hidden in his hand. Marcel is standing by Albertine, and at one moment she looks at him with an air of complicity. It is only about the game – but he sees in the look a vast landscape of possible complicity stretching out. He fumbles his moves with the ring in his preoccupation, and she shouts angrily at him. He is stricken with grief. But the look full of promise, followed immediately by its loss, are what propel him into love.

Now he becomes even more aware of the many-sidedness of Albertine. It is not only a question of her character, but even of her face: grey and thin one day; or white and glossy, with an elusive pink in the cheeks; or bathed by happiness with a kind of transparent clarity. But he also begins to dissimulate his love for her – and indeed through all that follows, he never declares to her that he loves her. He believes, after his experience with Gilberte, that he will bind her to him the more strongly this way.

Whether he does or not, we never know, because we never get a clearer, more stable picture of Albertine than Marcel receives. This is one of the most remarkable of Proust's achievements. He keeps our interest alive in a love-affair that occupies hundreds of pages and is full of detailed analysis of the man's feelings, without allowing us ever to reach any conclusions about the woman's feelings, and not many more about her behaviour. The Albertine story enables us to experience for ourselves the idea that so frequently presents itself to Marcel: that you cannot see clearly a person who excites your emotions, and especially your love – and by so much the more so, the more intense and obsessive your love is.

Marcel's experience with Albertine is mainly one of suffering.

From their first kiss, she seems to be escaping from him. This kiss takes place not, as he had hoped, in the hotel at Balbec, but later in his family's flat in Paris. As his lips approach her cheek, he says, 'it was ten Albertines I saw' (II P365, K379). Her face, getting closer and closer, is like a series of photographs, all showing us a group of familiar buildings in strange new relationships and perspectives. Nevertheless, the couple embark on a somewhat obscure sexual liaison, and almost at once Marcel's suspicions and fears begin to gather.

He goes through the same set of feelings about her again and again. When he starts imagining that she is interested in another man, he feels a deep need to bind her to him, to hear her soothing reassurances, which he is always willing to believe. But as soon as he has these reassurances, he feels rather bored with her, even trapped by her: a longing comes on him to go out into society, and meet other women. Then suspicions start up in him again, and once more he is exclusively obsessed with controlling her. Moreover, his anguish is a double one. It is not only a question of the torment he feels when he is in the grip of suspicion and jealousy. He also suffers, and still more deeply, from the impulse he has to seek other women when he is sure of her. These are the 'intermittencies of the heart' to the contemplation of which the novel keeps returning – a phrase that Proust thought at one time of using as its title (II P751, K778). The fact that he has these disjunctions of feeling disturbs Marcel's whole sense of himself as a single being, continuous in the element of time. When he thinks of breaking off with Albertine, it is as much because he cannot bear this feeling of discontinuity in his own nature, as because he cannot bear the pain of jealousy.

The situation becomes even more unbearable one night at Balbec when he is watching her dancing with another girl from the 'little band'. Dr Cottard, one of Mme Verdurin's 'regulars', makes a sly joke about the evident sexual attraction of the two girls for each other, and at once another nightmarish world of threats presents itself to Marcel: perhaps Albertine's infidelity to him has not been with men, but with women. His jealous sufferings become greater than ever, and he is just about to announce that he is making a final break with her, when she casually remarks that she knows the daughter of the composer, Vinteuil.

Now years before, as a small boy, Marcel had spied on this girl, who lived at Combray. He had seen her and another girl, the two of them clearly lovers, proposing to spit on the photograph of Vinteuil the father, now dead. It was an act of sadism and lasciviousness that had made a profound impression on him. Hearing that Albertine knows Vinteuil's daughter, he is finally convinced of her Lesbianism. He decides that she must never leave him again, and sweeps her off to Paris to live with him in the flat, from which his mother and father are away.

The volume called *La prisonnière*, which describes their life together in the flat, contains the most haunting pages about their relationship. Marcel finds a kind of calm – above all, when he is watching Albertine sleep. In the light of what we know about Marcel, we can see why this is. Sleeping in his own home, she gives herself to him without any word or look of hers doing anything to disturb or confuse him. 'She had called back into herself everything of her that lay outside,' he says. What she meant for him from the beginning at Balbec is caught in the sound of her breathing – 'a murmuring, mysterious emanation, soft as a sea breeze' (III P70, K64). In some ways, there is an even better moment for him when she first wakes. He watches her eyes open: she recognises that she is in *his* room – and she relaxes. This is another moment of pure, unmarred peace for Marcel.

But in the daytime there is still plenty of anguish and anxiety for him. He stays indoors, often in bed because of his asthma; but she must go out. Her friend Andrée goes as her chaperone – but he has constantly renewed fears that Albertine and Andrée have sexual relations. Yet he can often reassure himself just through a confirmation that she will return. On the day which takes up most of the action of *La prisonnière*, Albertine goes out to the Trocadéro. Later in the day, Marcel sees in the newspaper that a Lesbian actress whom Albertine might know is performing at the theatre there. He immediately sends Françoise out to fetch her back. Then, in the usual way, once Françoise has telephoned to say they are returning, he completely forgets

Albertine and his thoughts go ranging far away from her.

That night, having persuaded Albertine to stay at home, he goes to the Verdurins at their new Paris house. His reason for not taking her with him is that he believes Vinteuil's daughter will be there. As it happens, he is wrong about this. But it proves to be a very important evening for him, as well as an intensely fascinating one: he hears a piece of music by Vinteuil which restores his flagging faith in art, and he witnesses Mme Verdurin break up the love-affair between Charlus and Morel. When Marcel goes home from the party he stands looking up at his window, behind which he knows he will find Albertine. The electric light, through the shutters, stripes it with gold. This window becomes the metaphor of his whole relationship with Albertine. It is like luminous gates, guarding his treasure for him in his own home. Yet these gates are made of 'inflexible bars of gold' which he has forged for his own 'eternal slavery', forfeiting 'his freedom, his solitude and his thought' (III P331, K336–7).

Nevertheless, the slavery is not eternal. For Albertine leaves him. Why she leaves him, we no more understand than we understand why she came to live with him. Of course, we can see his charm, his intelligence, his wealth, his learning; we can also see what a tiresome lover he must have been. None of this enables us to grasp Albertine's real motives, because Marcel, twist and turn his thoughts as he may, with an extraordinary plenitude of imaginings and suppositions, never feels he has grasped them either. He tries to discover where she has gone and to bring her back; but even at this stage, whenever he thinks she is going to return, his feeling of boredom with her and his rest-lessness attack him afresh. She is killed in a riding accident; and the months and years of reconciliation to her loss begin. But now a new 'intermittency' fills Marcel with pain: the knowledge that he is, slowly, forgetting her. His grief fades; and the loss of that grief becomes a matter for deeper grief. At the end, all he is left with is suffering, and what he can draw from it for his art.

Homosexuality and bisexuality

Two other lovers of particular importance in *A la recherche* are Robert de Saint-Loup and the Baron de Charlus. As we have seen, when Marcel first meets him, Robert is passionately in love with Rachel, and Marcel gets another startling revelation of the subjectivity of love. It took Robert a long time, it seems, to persuade Rachel, now starting as an actress, to become his mistress; whereas Marcel could have had her at the first brothel he ever visited, and did not want her. 'What to me had been offered at the start,' he says, 'had been for Robert an ultimate goal towards which he had made his way through endless hopes and doubts.' He also reflects, in the same vein as his thoughts about Swann and Odette, 'how much a human imagination can put behind a little scrap of a face' (II P159, K161). The application of this remark to his own love for Albertine will not escape him, in due course.

There is also a sleep scene in Robert's life which foreshadows Marcel's experiences in the Paris flat in a comic and touching way. After Rachel has deserted Robert, she will sometimes come back for convenience for a bed for the night. It gives Robert a profound satisfaction that, on those nights, her body still remembers the movements of his body and that, if he is restless, she does not wake up, 'even if he took up the greater part of the bed himself' (II P349, K362). It may be a meagre kind of possession of her in her sleep, but it is very important to him. Robert eventually becomes – or shows himself to have been since long before – a homosexual. But we do not see much of this later life of his, most of which comes to Marcel by hearsay. Robert marries Gilberte but neglects her, and his last passion before he is killed in the Great War is Morel, Charlus's ex-lover.

Charlus is the fullest study Proust gives us of a homosexual lover. Like Robert, and unlike Marcel, he is very decisive in the way he conducts his love-affairs. He first sees Morel on the railway station at Doncières. He falls in love with him on the spot, and immediately changes all his travel plans in order to set about this new conquest. But he, too, is almost totally self-deceived. He tries to persuade Morel to renounce society for him, when the ambitious young violinist has hardly taken his first step into it. Naturally Charlus is quite unsuccessful. When he is jealous of Morel, he tries to bring him to heel with the kind of rage that might have worked with an upper-class boy, but has no effect at all on this son of Marcel's uncle's valet. He never sees clearly what a vain, insecure, suggestible person Morel is, and so he loses him, to his amazement and to his despair.

There are several long disquisitions on homosexuality in *A la recherche*, and the main argument in them is that the homo-sexual, even more than the heterosexual lover, has to live a life of delusion. Proust is writing especially of those male homo-sexuals who, like Charlus, are attracted only by virile young men of heterosexual appetites. Naturally, they never find a man who is both to their taste and able to return their love. A brilliantly comic development of this idea comes in the description of the male brothel in *Le temps retrouvé*. Charlus, now growing old, is whipped and beaten there by young men who are presented to him as being criminals or butchers, or as doing 'filthy things' with their wives, in order to provide the extra thrill and fear which will give him his masochistic orgasm (III P827, K856). But from their conversation, which Marcel overhears, we discover that they are perfectly normal, and normally married, young men, who have just come to the brothel to do a job. Even Charlus is half-aware that this is so; but he wants to be deceived.

We have at this point to confront a major question about *A la recherche*. One might just regard Charlus as a realistic study of a homosexual, and the other references to homosexuals in the book as forming simply a background to him, an evocation of the homosexual milieu, just as the other major characters all have their background. But this does not seem an adequate response to the homosexual element in the novel. In the first place, towards the end of the book many characters whom we have not suspected of being homosexual reveal that they are; or at any rate they become so. Saint-Loup is not the only example; Legrandin declares his homosexuality, so does the Prince de Guermantes. The English critic Malcolm Bowie has described the end of the book as a kind of 'comic millennium' for homo-sexuals. Proust seems here to be insisting on an important point for him — something more than a mere demonstration to ignorant readers that homosexuality is commoner than they think.

For we cannot separate this insistent note of the last part of the book from the most extraordinary feature of Marcel's love for Albertine – the fact that his greatest fears and suspicions are that she is having affairs with other women. Among heterosexual men, this must be a fairly rare anxiety. Yet it obsesses Marcel, without him having any real evidence that Albertine is like that at all. Proust builds up the evidence that she has Lesbian tendencies from innumerable sources, but if one goes through it carefully one sees that it is never conclusive. Every testimony that Marcel gets from other people on the matter is suspect for one reason or another – reasons that he himself is always able to give us. So whether Marcel's fears are justified or not we never know.

What we are learning, in fact, is something about him, not about her. It is his imagination that dwells perpetually on the question, to a quite ludicrous extent on occasion. For instance, after Albertine is dead, and he is with his mother in Venice, he meets a charming Austrian girl. Within minutes, because of certain mild resemblances she has to Albertine – a fresh complexion and a light-hearted manner – he is wondering if she is a Lesbian.

Why did Proust attribute this obsession to Marcel, among all the other difficulties he has in his relationships with people? It must be of some relevance that Proust himself was, in part, homosexual; and that his account of Marcel's love for Albertine can be shown to have certain affinities with his own strong attachment to a secretary and chauffeur who worked for him, Alfred Agostinelli. Some critics have plainly stated that in Marcel's love-affair with Albertine, we just get an account of a homosexual love-affair in disguise. In this case, Marcel's fear of Albertine having relationships with women is in fact a homosexual's fear of his boy-lover having such relationships.

There seem to be very good reasons for not accepting this argument. One would be that this does not seem to be an essential homosexual fear. No doubt certain homosexual men particularly hate the idea of their lovers also loving women, but there are many, perhaps a majority, for whom this does not present a major threat. Charlus himself is an example; he actually wants Morel to marry, provided he can exercise some power over Morel's wife, because that will enable him to keep Morel under closer surveillance. What Proust's own feelings were in this matter must remain a matter for speculation, but it is perhaps worth noting that Agostinelli was married, and that Proust let his wife live in with him, and helped her considerably after Agostinelli's death in a flying accident.

A far more weighty reason for doubting whether Proust was, as it were, palming a homosexual relationship off on us in disguise is the fact that he was, above all, an artist, and a supremely conscious and thorough one. *A la recherche* is not a novel in the vein of traditional realism, but in certain respects it strictly observes the conventions of realism: everything is done to make the characters lifelike, deeply involved in realistically observed milieux, consistent within themselves (which does not mean predictable) in every aspect of their behaviour. Writing a novel with that intention, Proust must surely have wanted us to regard his women as women, as one of the most basic elements in its truthfulness to life. Odette is a supremely womanly woman − Proust had no difficulty in achieving that. And though we never visualise Albertine as clearly as we do Odette, this, as we have seen, is necessary to the indirect portrayal we get of Marcel as the teller of the story. Whenever we do get a sharp impression of Albertine, she has the lineaments and manners of a girl, indeed a charming one. This is not to say that Proust did not incorporate some of his own experiences into the story of Marcel and Albertine; but he used them to create a portrait of a heterosexual love-affair. (George Painter, in fact, suggests that Proust's relationship with Alfred, rather than provide all the material for the Albertine story, at some points did the reverse and imitated in life what Proust had already conceived in art.)

A far more interesting and rewarding approach to the question opens up if we consider another point: namely, that most of the characters who have homosexual lovers have lovers of the other sex as well. They are bisexual, in fact. Even Charlus was once married, though perhaps that is one relationship we need not take too seriously. But with Saint-Loup, it is plainly spelt out that he is capable of feeling passion and desire for both men and women, possibly even at the same time.

This is perhaps coming nearer to the point Proust is insisting on. Besides all the other divisions in our nature, there is a further one – that in some form our desires are directed towards both the sexes. Into this suggestion it is easier to fit the case of Marcel. Marcel is almost exceptional among the characters in the book in that he shows no overt homosexual tendencies. What his preoccupations and habits indirectly bring out is that he does have some traits that we may call bisexual. We are dealing here with obscure depths of the mind, where nothing is very clear; nevertheless it is here that we may find some explanation of his obsession with Albertine's suspected homosexuality. Either he is attributing to her alarming and repressed homosexual tendencies of his own, appropriately transposed to fit the fact that she is a girl; or, while fearing them, he is wishing on her certain feelings that would bring her closer to being a boy. By their nature, these are emotions that it is impossible to inspect closely in life; while in fiction, the concealed desires of an imaginary character created by a dead author seem as remote from human investigation as any human characteristics could be. Looked at in this light, however, Marcel's and Albertine's personalities remain acceptable within the canons of psychological realism, without the couple ceasing to be the young man and women they so palpably are.

These 'bisexual' tendencies of Marcel's are expressed, if we read them aright, in subtle ways. We may illustrate them from two episodes already mentioned. It was noted that when Marcel was being comforted by his grandmother in Balbec, she herself found an 'exquisite pleasure' in anticipating the repose she would bring him. Does this not strangely resemble the pleasure Marcel takes in watching Albertine sleeping? When he is doing that, he is indeed, as we have seen, drawing deep repose from the fact that he has her exclusively to himself, as he wanted his mother as a child. But he is also the watching, guarding one, like his mother, like his grandmother, watching over a sleeping child – a child who we may think resembles himself, as a young boy, in his imagination. If this is so, his inner calm is understandably of a peculiarly deep kind: for his masculine and his feminine impulses are both being gratified simultaneously — indeed, are united — in his vigil. But when Albertine gets up and resumes her life as an independent being again, he becomes once more like all the other lovers. They too are united, no matter what their varied sexual tendencies — but united only in their inescapable misery, in their hopeless quest for lasting peace.

4 Marcel and his ideas

Marcel's observations

We have now looked at Marcel's personality as it reveals itself in his fascination with society and his successive experiences of love. But its presence is of course pervasive throughout the book: every observation he makes expresses it. His sense of the perpetual alternation of loss and recovery in human existence goes back, as we have seen, to his childhood; but it is not only a question of his own experiences with his mother and grand-mother. He finds the same thing taking place in almost everyone he observes around him. However, when he is a child, obser-vation of others is for him a continuous pleasure, even if mixed with his private anxieties; and that capacity for pleasure in the world continues throughout his life. Lying awake in the early morning, when he is living with Albertine but she is still asleep in the next room, he thinks to himself that the 'person' who lies deepest in him is a 'little mannikin' who, when he realises that dawn is breaking, sends up a hymn to the glory of the sun (III P12, K4). That 'little mannikin' who loves the world never vanishes from *A la recherche*, and his murmurs of laughter and enjoyment reach us from most of the pages of Marcel's narrative.

One of the first vivid impressions Marcel has of the unpredict-able coming and going of feelings is a story his grandfather likes to tell about Swann's father, at the time when Swann's mother died. Marcel's grandfather 'managed to entice M. Swann for a moment, weeping profusely, out of the death-chamber' – and then, as they walked in the sunshine, suddenly old M. Swann seized Marcel's grandfather by the arm and cried 'How fortu-nate we are to be walking here together on such a charming day! ... Whatever you may say, it's good to be alive!' Then abruptly the memory of his dead wife came back to him, and he rubbed his hand across his forehead in perplexity that he had spoken like that (I P15, K15–16).

Almost all Marcel's anecdotes about people have this dual character. They bring the person dramatically to life, in all his inimitable individuality — but they always, in the end, refer back to the great themes of the book, which are one and the same as the obsessions of Marcel the narrator.

These intermittencies that haunt Marcel have their inner and their outer aspects. The story of old M. Swann is registered by Marcel mainly as a matter of inner inconsistency. But it also contains an element of erratic perception of the outer world — a feature of human behaviour that Marcel observes throughout his childhood, in Françoise, the family servant. At Combray, when the kitchen-maid, soon after having a baby, is stricken with appalling pains, Françoise is sent to fetch a medical dictionary which will tell Marcel's mother what first aid the girl needs. Françoise starts reading about the after-pains, and for an hour sobs and prays over the book at the idea of such agonies. But she completely forgets the suffering girl she is supposed to be helping. Again, when Marcel's grandmother is dying, Françoise is willing to stay up night after night to keep her company. But she also insists on combing the old woman's straggling grey hair to make it look better, regardless of the pain it causes her. In both cases, Françoise's acts fail to connect in any rational or useful way with the needs of the person they are meant to serve. Inner preoccupations inhibit her, for a time, from any genuine imaginative reaching out to the reality of the kitchen-maid or Marcel's grandmother.

Marcel's instability

In Marcel's own life, such experiences take many and complex forms. The root of them all is a feeling of profound psychological instability. His own nature is all the time undergoing changes that make it hard for him to retain any sense of himself as a coherent being. And the outer world is equally unstable. Other people, especially, seem to be in a constant state of flux — and he cannot even tell if it is they who are changing, or if it is simply his own perceptions that are so incoherent and unreliable. After Albertine is dead, he reflects that she seems to be just as alive to him as before, because he still retains all the varied impressions of her that he used to recall when she was really alive. To feel that she was dead, he says, 'what I should have to annihilate in myself was not one, but innumerable Albertines'. But 'it was not Albertine alone who was a succession of moments, it was also myself ... I was not one man only, but as it were the march-past of a composite army in which there were passionate men, indifferent men, jealous men – jealous men not one of whom was jealous of the same woman' (III P488–9, K498–9).

Marcel is not passive in this situation. In the first place, although the multiplicity of experience confuses and distresses him, it is not a question of his wanting all its intransigent individual bits to vanish. On the contrary, he wants a wealth of emotion; he adores the many aspects of Albertine; he is glad that the world is full of girls. What he needs is to hold them all in some coherent and unified relation with each other, and with himself.

And he has strategies for doing this. One which we have seen already is his impulse to brood on the name rather than the reality of a person or a place, and let its historical or mythical associations dominate his thought. It gives him, often, a quite exciting or glamorous hold on the world. But of course it is always a useless strategy in the end. The reality – as when he visits Balbec, as when he meets the Guermantes – always shatters the word-image eventually. Complexity and confusion return, and Marcel seems to be left with the stark choice: illusion or division.

There is a still further complication. Illusion itself may be a cause of division. As so often, we are given a ludicrous example of the point. The lift-boy at Balbec persists in calling the Marquise de Cambremer 'the Marquise de Camembert' (II P825, K854). He cannot be budged from the idea because he can see nothing wrong with the name. On the contrary, it satisfies his sense of rightness: it is not surprising that a marquisate should be named after such a great cheese. Marcel's 'Guermantes', we might say, is the lift-boy's 'Camembert'. Both names satisfy their users' desire for coherence and unity. But both the young men are victims, while they think like that, of an illusion that separates them from the reality of the Guermantes or the Cambremers. In fact, they are very like Françoise, when her fascinated absorption in an idea of suffering or neatness blinds her to the facts about Marcel's grandmother or the kitchen-maid.

Marcel's own awareness of this problem comes out very clearly in his thoughts about the fact that various girls to whom he is attracted are rather like each other. On the one hand, that seems to offer him a prop to his sense of continuity in his nature, something he greatly desires. On the other hand, it suggests that he is not seeing and responding to the girls wholly and distinctly as individuals, something that he also wants. Indeed, at those times when it is novelty and adventure rather than solace and peace that beckon him, it is precisely the mys-teriousness of new women that he longs for — such as the feeling, in a strange place, that though he is only three feet from a passing girl, she seems to be 'separated from him by the impossible' (III P989, K1038). To complete this paradox, he suggests at another moment in the story that it is only when a woman is new and mysterious that a man can know anything about her at all, because once she becomes familiar and he begins to have feelings about her, complexity and confusion start up again. And all the other intermittencies follow in the wake of that — the desire (familiar by now to the reader) to know and control, and the impulse once more to escape.

Marcel's sense of unity

With women, these are dilemmas that Marcel never resolves. But, on a quite simple level, he does have an eye for a comfort-ing unity when he meets it in the world. Moreover, even as a child he has intuitions of some real possibility of keeping the objects in his world distinct and yet related, both in space and time.

When he visits the Swanns' house, at the time he is in love with Gilberte, he sees in their drawing-room a harmony that, objectively, it certainly does not have. Among Odette's Chinese ornaments, probably fakes, there are new chairs and stools draped in Louis XVI silks; and Swann has brought in a Rubens from his old house. But because of the charm in which his imagination had for so long bathed the life of the Swann family, 'it has kept in my memory,' says Marcel, 'that composite, heterogeneous room, a cohesion, a unity, an individual charm ... for we alone, by our belief, can give to certain things we see a soul' (I P539, K580–1). When he is staying in Balbec for the second time, he gets to know the little coastal train that runs from Balbec, via Doncières, Saint-Loup's garrison town, out to La Raspelière, where the Verdurins are staying. This train draws the whole of this part of Normandy into a unity, visible to the traveller as he passes. When the train stops at each station, all the country gentry who live around are to be found there, just waiting for a brief chat with friends who are passing by. Marcel knows many of them by now, and he sees the railway line as a long chain of friendships, with the train itself presiding over them, patient and kind.

The most important experience of this kind in his youth is, however, of a different order, and without his knowing it at the time, it points his way ahead to his work as a writer. At this period of his life, such things as the gleam of sunlight on a stone, or the smell of a path, often give him strange feelings of a greater fecundity in the world, a deeper meaning in it, than he usually has. One day he has a particularly strong sensation of this kind. He is riding on the box of the Combray doctor's carriage, and suddenly he sees the twin steeples of Martinville, 'bathed in the setting sun and constantly changing their position with the movement of the carriage and the windings of the road' (I P180, K196). Then a third steeple joins them, that of the village of Vieuxvicq. Later, driving on from Martinville, he sees them again, still changing position all the time in relation to each other, black now in the dusk.

Georges Poulet, the Belgian critic, has expressed very well the significance this experience has for Marcel. It is not 'a vacillating or whirling of landscape,' he says, 'but liberated elements use their newly acquired mobility to bring themselves together and form a new creation'. It makes a sharp contrast with the feeling Marcel more often has about places — namely, to quote Poulet again, that 'the mobility of places takes away our last anchor'. What is especially to the point is that Marcel has this experience just after he has been thinking, rather desperately, that he has no hope of a literary career. At this time, he supposes that to be a writer one needs philosophical themes and abstract truths, in which he seems to be conspicuously lacking. He doesn't immediately see the Martinville steeples as offering a sign to him, a promise and a prophecy that he will create literature of another kind. Nevertheless, the experience impels him to write a page about it, which he does with pencil and paper borrowed from the doctor, as he is jolted about on the way home to Combray. He is so pleased when he has done this that he begins to sing at the top of his voice.

The young Marcel may not grasp the point, but Proust is making it plain to us. The experience certainly has something to do with Marcel's literary future. In fact, it not only tells us that he is going to be an artist, but also gives us a clear hint of what his art will be like.

The fictitious artists: Bergotte, Elstir, Vinteuil

From a very early age, Marcel cherishes the dream of being a writer. He has done his reading, of course – his Racine, his Balzac, his Baudelaire. But in his teens he is particularly attracted to a contemporary writer, Bergotte. Bergotte is an invention of Proust's, supposedly based on the novelist and critic, Anatole France (though France's essentially rationalist, commonsensical work has not much in common with Bergotte's writings). Marcel gets his first encouragement to be a writer from M. de Norpois, a diplomat, his father's friend and superior. But he is confused and dismayed when Norpois goes on to disparage Bergotte. Norpois believes that literature should deal in 'lofty conceptions'; for him, Bergotte, with his fastidious attention to form, is a mere 'flute-player' (I P473–4, K510–11).

Marcel, as we have seen, also thinks when he is very young that 'lofty conceptions', soaring philosophical thoughts, are what a writer should aspire to. But it is through the influence of writers like Bergotte that he modifies these ideas. When he meets Bergotte at the Swanns', he has to jettison other false notions too, for Bergotte as a man is not remotely like the 'stalactite' that Marcel had elaborated for himself, 'drop by drop, out of the transparent beauty of his books' (I P547, K589). He is squat, with a snail-shell nose. But as Marcel listens to his voice, which intones rather than speaks the words, he sees clearly something in Bergotte's work that even Bergotte's admirers often miss. They value him — just like Norpois in their own way — for his 'Bergottisms', his remarkable thoughts. What Marcel sees is something quite different: 'a plastic beauty, independent of whatever his sentences might mean' (I P550, K592 3). Whether Marcel, or Proust, would in the end have stood by such a strictly formal account of the beauty of prose, I think we must doubt. But for Marcel, at this point, it is a liberation from the idea that the intellect is the chief organ of literary creation.

We last see Bergotte on the day of his death, which is actually the reverberating day when Marcel goes to the Verdurins' party and leaves Albertine in the flat. Bergotte dies in an art gallery, where, already very ill, he has dragged himself to look at Vermeer's *View of Delft*. His last act is to contemplate a fine detail in the painting a little yellow patch of wall. He collapses as he studies it, thinking 'I have given away my life for this'. Literally, of course, he means that by coming out to see it he has killed himself. But symbolically we must take him to mean that he has sacrificed his life to the precisions and beauties of art. Proust himself went to see this very painting not long before he died, and wrote this passage after his visit; so I think we must suppose that he was talking of himself here, with just the mingled feelings that Bergotte has. Yet, with one of those endless twists and accretions of implication that we find in *A la recherche*, Bergotte also reflects, in his last thoughts, that his works have not been as rich as that little patch of yellow: 'My last books are too dry, I ought to have gone over them with a few layers of colour' (III P187, K185).

We can hear Proust's voice here again. He admired the dedication of writers such as Bergotte, and the exquisite quality of their work; but in the role of Marcel he would go over his work with many layers of colour, for reasons deeper than Bergotte ever began to know.

Two other fictitious artists are important to Marcel. One is the painter, Elstir, whom he meets at Balbec. Something of what Marcel finds in Elstir's landscapes and seascapes gets into *A la recherche*. He says that Elstir created his work out of 'the rare moments when we see nature as she is, poetically': Elstir tried to 'strip himself of every intellectual notion' and come 'face to face with reality'. God gave things names, says Marcel, but Elstir took them away again (I P835, 840, K893–4, 898).

These are ideas drawn from the Impressionist painters, especially Renoir and Monet. Later critics have questioned both the philosophical and the optical soundness of the notion that there is any such thing as a raw, true impression unmodified by the mind, arguing that there are, rather, just different ways in which we choose to see things. However, the principle certainly helped the Impressionist artists to produce paintings in which the beauty of shifting lights and colours was caught as never before; and the psychological self-portrait drawn by Marcel uses the same ideas very effectively. It certainly shows us how 'names' and 'intellectual notions' can deceive us; and, in illustrative contrast, it tries to give us Marcel's 'impressions' as they truly come to him, abundant, fresh and unworked-on. The permanent confusion in Marcel's view of Albertine belongs to this aspect of his self-portrait – as does another curious detail, the fact that we never know Marcel's age at any point. Consciousness of our age in numbers of years, Proust would undoubtedly say, is one of those 'intellectual notions' that is never part of our immediate perception of the world.

The third artist is the composer, Vinteuil. He is an old music teacher who lives in Combray. After his death, the only finished composition he leaves is a sonata, which provides another beautifully drawn connection between Swann and Marcel. Swann hears the sonata played at the Verdurins' when he is in love with Odette. One phrase in particular haunts him, and for a while he is convinced that music 'is on an equal footing with the ideas of the intellect'. Proust here anticipates, but with a touch of delicate comedy at Swann's expense, Marcel's own discovery, through Bergotte and Elstir and Vinteuil, of the supremacy of art over all other human activities. Swann even thinks, at the time, that in the company of Vinteuil's phrase 'death would be less bitter' (I P350, K380–1). But later he forgets what he has felt, and only retains a vague, sentimental memory of pleasure in the music.

Marcel is to receive far more enduring impressions from Vinteuil's work. He, too, comes to love the sonata; nevertheless, while listening to Albertine playing it for him on the pianola, he is beset by some of his deepest doubts about leading the life of an artist. He suddenly has a feeling that art offers nothing better than life, that it does not reflect any special power or insight on the part of the artist; that the artist is merely a labourer who contrives to give us a different, but not superior pleasure.

However, at the Verdurin party – the same one that keeps recurring here, the one he goes to from the Paris flat – he hears another work of Vinteuil's, a septet (supposedly based on a work of César Franck's). There is an extraordinary irony for Marcel in the very existence of this work. It has been painstakingly put together, from notes that Vinteuil left, by that very friend of Vinteuil's daughter who once wanted to spit on Vinteuil's portrait, and whose imagined relations with Albertine have been the cause of Marcel's greatest anguish. This nameless girl, on this climactic day, brings Marcel a restored and henceforth imperishable sense of the unique meaning and glory of art, as he listens to the septet she herself has restored.

Marcel's ideas about art

What, then, does Marcel come to think about the nature of art, as he approaches the time when he will begin writing? Many of his thoughts on this subject arise as he is listening to Vinteuil's music, and one point that particularly recurs is the idea that art gives us a unique revelation of another person's actual experience of the world. This, we might say, is the subjective complement of what he has found in Elstir's painting, where the stress was more on the authenticity of the objective element – the direct impression of nature as it really is. In Marcel's thought, the two become essentially indivisible, and represent all that we can, in any rewarding sense, 'know'.

The idea comes to him when he is playing Vinteuil's sonata on the piano: 'As the spectrum makes visible to us the composition of light, so the harmony of a Wagner, the colour of an Elstir, enable us to know that essential quality of another person's sensations into which love for another person does not allow us to penetrate' (III P159, K156). Later, listening to the septet at Mme Verdurin's, he carries the thought further. It seems to him that in all Vinteuil's music there is audible a 'voice', a 'song', that is different from every other composer's, and is always recognisable. The same is true of every other genuinely original composer; and this 'unique accent' is 'a proof of the irreducibly individual existence of the soul' (III P256, K258).

Where does the composer learn this song? By way of answer, Marcel imagines that every artist brings his individual song from a lost and forgotten fatherland, to which he draws nearer and nearer again as his work develops, taking us with him. He concludes that for us, the only true voyage of discovery is not to foreign lands, but 'to see the universe through the eyes of another, of a hundred others, to see the hundred universes that each of them sees, that each of them is; and this we can do with an Elstir, with a Vinteuil' (III P258, K260). He contrasts this real possibility with the repeated fiasco of his attempts to understand living people directly: speaking of one 'caressing' phrase of Vinteuil's, he says, making the most explicit of comparisons, 'this phrase – this invisible creature – is perhaps the only Unknown Woman that it has ever been my good fortune to meet' (III P260, K262).

We can consider these ideas of Marcel's from two points of view. First, we might feel that they express a very specialised and limited view of what art offers us. Nevertheless, the idea that true art springs from the authentic personal sensibility of its creator has been very pervasive in twentieth-century criticism – a reflection of our loss of absolute certitudes. Even a critic such as F. R. Leavis, who stressed the moral wisdom and civilising power of great art, both of them qualities of wide-ranging importance, insisted that such art has its origins in some 'vital' personal experience, that it grows 'organically' out of the 'whole being' of the artist.

More particularly, we can see how happily such a view of art answers to Marcel's own anxieties. If he can 'meet' another person fully and reliably in art, two supremely comforting solutions offer themselves to his fears. First, he has at last, in the art of others, a chance of discovering some stability in the world around him. Even more important, if he can become an artist himself, he can overcome his own haunting sense of inner instability. He may at last be able to create something in which his own personality will be locked firm, and made accessible to mankind.

All the same, if this idea of art inspires Marcel, it does not immediately solve any of the problems. Has he himself a 'lost fatherland'? Has he a 'self' at all? If so, how can he find it? And even if he can, what possible form might his art take?

The steeples of Martinville continue to hold out one hope to him. In fact, the article he publishes in *Le Figaro* – the one that the Duke cannot believe in – is a reworking of the thoughts about the steeples that he wrote in the jolting carriage as a boy. It is his first literary success. Nor has he finished with the steeples after that. They come into his mind again as he listens to a joyous phrase in Vinteuil's septet:

> I knew that this tone of joy . . . was a thing I would never forget. But would it ever be attainable to me? This question seemed all the more important inasmuch as this phrase was what seemed most eloquently to characterise . . . those impressions which at remote intervals I experienced in my life as starting-points, foundation-stones for the construction of a true life: the impression I had felt at the sight of the steeples of Martinville, or of a line of trees near Balbec (III P261, K262–3).

Intimations of the kind of unity he needs, both for his life and his art, come to him also in dreams, when they reawaken in him 'something of the desire for certain non-existent things which is the necessary condition for working, for freeing oneself from the dominion of habit' (III P914, K953). But the main agent which keeps suggesting itself to him as a means of drawing his life together in a unity that would serve as the basis for his art, is memory.

Memory brings us back, at last, to the *madeleine*. We read about the little piece of cake dipped in tea at the very beginning of *A la recherche*. We are not told when the incident happened: all we know is that it must have been some time in Marcel's middle years. The experience brought back the past for him, but, as far as we are told, it did not at the time have the meaning for his art that later experiences of the same kind reveal. Implicitly, of course, Marcel (and Proust) are looking ahead to that meaning. But here, at the start of the book, Proust is just showing us a vivid 'involuntary memory' in action, and, without further elaboration, following it with an account of the world remembered – the world of Combray. Combray springs into being again like Japanese paper flowers when they are dropped in water – 'stretching and twisting and taking on colour and distinctive shape, becoming flowers or houses or people, solid and recognisable' (I P47, K51).

The full meaning of the *madeleine* is revealed at the other end of the book, when in its last pages Marcel arrives at the home of the new Princesse de Guermantes, an elderly man himself meeting aged friends again. He is dejected; he has spent much of the war in a sanatorium, and is feeling that all his responsiveness to the world has left him, and his dream of being a writer will never now come true. Then, in quick succession, he has an amazing series of sensations.

He trips over some uneven paving-stones, and recovers his balance by putting his foot on a lower stone. Suddenly, as he does this, he has a dazzling vision of Venice, where he had once done just the same thing in the baptistery of St Mark's. A moment later, he hears a servant knocking a spoon against a plate – and equally suddenly he finds himself back in the railway carriage on his recent return journey to Paris, looking out now with a feeling of extraordinary happiness at a line of trees, with sunlight flooding their crests. The connection here in his memory was the sound of a railwayman tapping a wheel with his hammer. Then he has a third, similar experience. The stiff, starchy feel of a napkin recalls a towel he dried his face with, standing at the window on his first day in Balbec – and the napkin unfolds for him, from within its smooth surfaces, 'the plumage of an ocean green and blue like the tail of a peacock' (III P869, K901).

These moments are the climax of the novel — and describe its birth. For in them, not only is Marcel's faith restored — his faith in his capacity both for joy and for creation — but also he sees what his novel must be. In these moments, his sensation of the world comes back to him with all its freshness and poetic force, not clouded by the anxieties and desires that accompanied such sensations at the time he first had them. What is more, these sensations comprise within themselves a wealth of other, allusive sensations — evocations of innumerable other, associated experiences, all revived in the same instant. This, Marcel perceives with absolute clarity, is what must become the substance of his creation: his own life, relived with this ecstasy, this many-layered richness, this purity of contemplation, and this unity.

It was Time that had always seemed the principal enemy to him. The steady, obliterating passage of Time was the chief cause of that terrifying instability in himself and the world. But now Time suddenly appears as the saviour, if he can confront and master it. For Lost Time also contains all that we have lived through, and so, he thinks, contains also our true or essential self. Once we have recovered Time, through memory and art, we are freed from its destructive power — we are outside Time. But to do this we must follow the clues offered us by such experiences of 'involuntary' memory as those he has just experienced. Deliberate, willed attempts to recapture the past leave us only with desiccated, isolated impressions. But Marcel's experiences with the uneven paving-stones, the clinking spoon and the napkin show us how it is possible to bring the whole of our past life together. They tell us not to look outside, but within ourselves, where the true and enduring self and the work of art both lie hidden, waiting for us — and are, moreover, for the artist who can bring them forth, identical. That is why so-called 'realist' art, with its external preoccupations, is so shallow. There is no truth — and so no true art — attainable by man except what he can elicit from his own inner experience.

5 Marcel's art and Proust's art

So we come to *A la recherche*, the work itself. For Marcel writes his book — and it is, we are left to understand, the book we have. We have seen how he comes to his conception of the one book he might write, and how this conception responds to his powerful and curious emotional needs. But how far does his book actually embody these ideas that, after long preparation, flood into his mind at the last great party he describes? And insofar as the book does embody them, how far are they fruitful ideas?

I think we can say that those elements in *A la recherche* which are most distinctive and original do correspond, in certain ways, to the ideas that inspire Marcel. Those elements we will call 'Marcel's art'. But we shall see in a moment that there are equally important aspects of the book that Marcel does not say much about. Those we shall call 'Proust's art' — not forgetting that 'Marcel's art' is also part of Proust's.

For a vivid and beautiful introduction to the precise nature of 'Marcel's art' we can go back, as so often in this novel, to its early pages, where we shall find what we want prefigured in a quite different context. It is where Marcel tells us how his grandmother would choose pictures for his room when he was a boy. She always felt that presents should contain an instructive element; so she would buy him photographs of ancient buildings. But she did not really like the 'commercial banality' of photographs, so 'she attempted by a subterfuge to minimise it, to supplant it to a certain extent with what was art still, to introduce several "thicknesses" of art: instead of photographs of Chartres Cathedral or the Fountains of Saint-Cloud, she preferred to give me photographs of "Chartres Cathedral" after Corot, or the "Fountains of Saint-Cloud" after Hubert Robert, which were a stage higher in the scale of art' (I P40, K43). But even that did not really satisfy her; and she would try if she could to lay hands on old engravings of paintings of old buildings . . .

Marcel is affectionately teasing his grandmother here, and the incident stands in its own right as one of the most touching moments in the book. Yet the 'thicknesses' of art that his grandmother hankers after describe exactly the most distinctive element of all in the way Marcel composes his memoirs. We meet, in this notion, the essence of the great 'Proustian sentence'. For what characterises an enormous proportion of the sentences in *A la recherche* is the way in which, while making quite graphically their main statement, they overlay it with associated memories, with metaphor, with comparisons with works of art, and — invisible at the time, but subsequently to be revealed — with allusions to many later experiences and thoughts of Marcel's. Earlier we saw the rich overlays in Proust's description of the fountain that Marcel sees in the Princesse de Guermantes's garden. Now we can detect a slight, but utterly characteristic example of what we are speaking of, in the passage about Marcel's grandmother just quoted. For there we are given a silent glance ahead to that very fountain — which was, it may be remembered, by that selfsame Hubert Robert whose picture of some fountains was sought by Marcel's grandmother as a present for him. The allusion goes like a whiplash across the thousand pages, binding the moments together and adding yet a further touch of drama to the revelation Marcel gets from the fountain.

But further to that, the grandmother passage as a whole operates on our imagination in at least three ways, apart from its simple, intrinsic interest. Like the Hubert Robert detail in it, it links up across the pages of the book with those other passages where Marcel's thoughts about his art are mentioned or alluded to. With even larger implications, it refers to and symbolises the very nature of the book it is in. And while doing all this, it is itself an example, in practice, of the very layers of 'thickness' that it is both comically and symbolically describing. In the act of reading it, we are not only being pointed to Marcel's ideas about art, but simultaneously experiencing the application of them. This is exactly the kind of complex weaving that Marcel, in his sudden flood of insights in *Le temps retrouvé*, sees as a means of overcoming time, and, in doing so, creating an art that will be unique and wholly personal.

We will just look briefly at two of Proust's sentences. Both of them concern women – it is noticeable that women especially excite an imaginative response in Marcel, whatever Proust's own later sexual impulses may have been. In the first, he describes the pretty hands of Andrée, Albertine's friend:

> Those of Andrée, slender and far more delicate, had as it were a private life of their own, obedient to the commands of their mistress, but independent, and used often to stretch out before her like thoroughbred greyhounds, with lazy pauses, languid reveries, sudden flexings of a finger-joint, seeing which Elstir had made a number of studies of these hands; and in one of them, in which Andrée was to be seen warming them at the fire, they had, with the light behind them, the golden diaphanousness of two autumn leaves. (I P919, K980)

Though shorter than many, it is a perfect example of a Proustian sentence, with its effect well preserved in the English version. From the literal physical description, it springs into metaphor – and in the very rhythm of the sentence we feel the greyhounds stretching out, even before they have been named, so that the reference to them seems to round off and confirm an impression in the act of surprising us; and we get a sense of spontaneity and controlled spaciousness at the same time. That is just what Proust wants, for the whole of his book and for every part of it. Still in the rhythm of the sentence, we seem to feel these lively and independent-minded greyhounds moving about – but then the very canine-like 'flexing' suddenly attaches itself to one of Andrée's finger-joints; and subject and metaphor are reunited in a way that is again both fresh, and restful with a sense of completion.

But still the sentence is not finished. It drops into a new key, as Marcel remembers that Elstir painted the hands – and the background to Marcel's friendship with Albertine and Andrée is brought to the fore again, with all Marcel's new passion for

Elstir's art. Then the thought (though not, to be strictly accurate, the sentence, since Proust puts a full stop after 'these hands') carries us on to an evocation of that painting, done at a different season, when hands are warmed before the fire. The passage of time now seems to threaten the hands. This sense of passing time continues into the next metaphor, which speaks plainly of autumn, the actual season of change and decay. Yet it brings us back, finally, to the present physical existence of Andrée's hands, and the beauty in them that arrests Marcel's attention. (All this, incidentally, is only by way of prelude to a description of Albertine's hands, and the still greater attraction that those have for him!)

The other sentence comes from the other end of the book, where Marcel describes the old women he meets at the Princess's party, and how they try to preserve their beauty. The description of Andrée's hands has anticipated change and age while dwelling on the hand's youthfulness; this superb sentence harks back to the beauty of youth through its powerful metaphor of age, and may even make us think of the fire before which Andrée's young hands were warming:

> But with few exceptions the women strained every nerve in a ceaseless struggle against old age and held out the mirror of their features towards beauty, as it receded, as to a setting sun whose last rays they longed passionately to preserve. (III P947, K989)

The metaphor of the mirror and the sun here seems to sweep into its compass a whole history of women's faces, and women's emotions about their faces — yet as an impression of an actual moment and gesture it is also absolutely right, if we think how a woman who knows her face is now lined will try to place it as directly as possible in the light, where its imperfections have a chance of being smoothed away.

Another device Proust uses to evoke the moments of Marcel's past, while drawing us into the larger sphere of his recollections, is the way in which Marcel will glide from the imperfect tense into the preterite (roughly, from 'used to do' to 'did') in the middle of a recollection. Memories that subsume various

occasions suddenly sharpen into the memory of a specific conversation or incident, which is then reabsorbed into the atmos-
phere or mood of a whole phase of Marcel's life. This device is
almost impossible to translate into English, which generally uses
the 'did' form for both meanings.

But how, one might ask, does Proust reconcile this feature of
the narrative with the ambition, expressed in the passages about
Elstir's art, to catch the artist's experience of the world in its
most immediate form, unworked on by the mind? How, to go
further, does he reconcile that ambition with the wealth of metaphor and comparison with which his sentences (as if it were
Bergotte putting into practice his dying thoughts) are loaded?

To put it shortly, the reconciliation is not complete. Nevertheless, Proust has already anticipated the question, and answered
it to a considerable degree, in his description of Elstir's work. It
will be remembered that Elstir is said to have created his work
out of 'the rare moments when we see nature as she is, poetically'. An enormous assumption is smuggled into that phrase.
But it is the final, underlying assumption of all Marcel's art, and
a very romantic one: namely that our authentic glimpses of the
world are poetic ones. If that is so, metaphor and comparison
are absolutely appropriate to our attempts to recreate those
fresh visions – fresh in the sense that they are undisturbed by
the ordinary thinking mind that in its dull, practical preoccupations and stock responses wipes the poetry away. In psychological terms, this fresh vision is in any event always subjective,
always composed both of what is there in the world, and of what
our emotions, with their trail of associations, link instan-
taneously to what we see and hear. Whether any of this is true
for humanity in general – whether, indeed, it is possible to
judge if it is true, or whether it is an assumption that cannot in
practice be put to the test – none of this strictly matters for
Proust the artist. The all-important thing is that this is the
assumption that allows Proust to create Marcel's art – what
Marcel offers us as his 'recollections' of 'nature as it is', in all
their beauty and intensity.

Precursors: Baudelaire, Bergson, Ruskin

It is not easy to find unmistakable precursors for Marcel's view of art, and for that aspect of the book that we have so far distinguished from the rest of it as 'Marcel's art'. Nor do we necessarily want to find any such influences! With a great, achieved work of art, original in every detail, it is difficult to say what an 'influence' really is, let alone to identify its presence in the work as evidence of something that actually took place in the author's mind when he was writing. But comparisons with other works may sometimes, at least, help us to see more clearly a feature of the work we are interested in; and Walter Benjamin makes a good case for thinking that Proust may have drawn some inspiration from the poet Charles Baudelaire.

Benjamin elaborates on a remark made by Marcel, where he says that experiences like his own with the *madeleine* are numerous in Baudelaire. 'The poet,' Marcel continues, 'with something of a slow and indolent choice, deliberately seeks, in the perfume of a woman, for instance, of her hair and her breast, the analogies which will inspire and evoke for him *l'azur du ciel immense et rond* (the azure of the vast, vaulted sky) and *un port rempli de flammes et de mâts* (a harbour full of flames and masts)' (III P920, K959). Walter Benjamin translates the word 'analogies' in this sentence (it is the same word in the French) as 'correspondences', suggesting that Proust was explicitly thinking here about Baudelaire's poem of that title ('*Correspondances*' in the original). In this poem, Baudelaire describes one of the main aims of his poetry: namely, to recognise and preserve those moments when 'scents, colours and sounds speak to each other, like long echoes that have come from afar and mingle in a deep shadowy unity, as vast as the night or the daylight':

> *Comme de longs echos qui de loin se confondent*
> *Dans une ténébreuse et profonde unité,*
> *Vaste comme la nuit et comme la clarté,*
> *Les parfums, les couleurs et les sons se répondent.*

We can certainly see similarities here between Baudelaire and Proust. The 'correspondences' that this verse describes and (in a

very Proustian way) at the same time gives us an experience of,
are, says Benjamin, 'experiences which seek to establish themselves in crisis-proof form'. In other words, they are moments
when we are not protecting ourself against the full inrush of our
experience, so we can take it in in all its richness. It is not
difficult to understand the appeal of that idea to Proust. But
Benjamin also brings out the significant differences between
Proust and Baudelaire. The 'moments' of the Baudelaire poems
appear to take us outside historical time; Baudelaire himself
gives them a distinctly mystical interpretation, suggesting they
may evoke memories of pre-existence, whereas Proust's attempt
to restore an existence in all its fullness remains within the limits
of earthly experience. If it can conquer time, it is only by an
exceptional degree of saturation in a life that is wholly temporal.

Another important influence on Proust was, it is often said,
his cousin by marriage, Henri Bergson, who was twelve years
older than him. As a young man, Proust heard Bergson's philosophical lectures at the Sorbonne. Bergson argued that there
were two sorts of time and two sorts of memory. There is our
conventional notion of time as a regular, external series of
divisions, just as there is our everyday memory, 'habit memory',
which we use in the practical conduct of our life. But much more
important to man are 'real' time, *la durée réelle*, time as we are
aware of it when we reflect on the full life of our consciousness;
and 'pure memory', which is the intuitive faculty with which we
do this.

As with Baudelaire, it is easy to see how these ideas would
have appealed to Proust. Yet it is not so easy to say that the
similarity of his own ideas means that he owed an intellectual
debt to Bergson. Here again, comparisons – and contrasts –
are illuminating, but 'influence' is hard to prove. Proust's
distinction between 'voluntary' and 'involuntary' memory is in
any event very different from Bergson's distinction between
'habit' and 'pure' memory. Bergson's 'pure' memory was by no
means dependent on chance associations suddenly opening up
lost stretches of the past.

On the other hand, we should perhaps ask how far Proust
really did draw on 'involuntary memory' to write *A la*

recherche. We do not in practice know anything about how he recovered his past; we cannot know in any detail how far his book actually relies on memory, and how far it is a work of imagination. The premise that the book is inspired by 'involuntary memory' is crucial to Marcel's story: it provides a great climax to the book, and gives the key to its scope and structure, as a history both intricate and joyous. 'Involuntary memory' is a dramatic way of suggesting all the most original qualities of this unprecedented novel. But we can scarcely believe that for twelve years Proust worked on his book drawing on no other internal resources. The novel tells us about everything that is supposed to have preceded the writing of the novel – but of that period of Marcel's life it tells us nothing. So we can say that Proust's published ideas on memory and art are different from Bergson's; but what his actual experience was in writing the novel we do not know at all.

John Ruskin's influence on *A la recherche* is perhaps a little more tangible. In his late twenties, Proust became a passionate admirer of Ruskin's work, responding with fervour and delight to his feeling for landscapes and Gothic churches, a response manifest enough in *A la recherche*. Proust's own first article in *Le Figaro* was in honour of Ruskin, and, as we have said, he translated *The Bible of Amiens* and *Sesame and Lilies*. But later he began to feel that Ruskin was too detached from people, as well as guilty of a rather ungenerous moralising whose connection with his aestheticism was far from clear. It was through his practical contact in translating Ruskin that Proust in the end learned most from him. Ruskin's long, impassioned sentences, pursuing a thought far afield while simultaneously flashing with brilliant pictures, are nearer to Proust's style in *A la recherche* than those of any other writer before him. In translating them, Proust had for the first time created such sentences in French.

Proust and Freud

There is one other contemporary of Proust who should perhaps be mentioned here, since in recent years comparisons have so often been made between them. This is Sigmund Freud. Proust often makes us think of Freud. He is alert as Freud was to the way in which people's inadvertent words can tell us something about their emotions that they are hardly aware of themselves. For years, says Marcel, 'I looked for the real life and thought of other people only in the direct statements about them which they supplied me with of their own free will'; but 'in the absence of these I had come to attach importance, on the contrary, only to disclosures that are not a rational and analytical expression of the truth; the words themselves did not enlighten me unless they were interpreted in the same way as a rush of blood to the cheeks of a person who is embarrassed, or as a sudden silence' (III P88, K83). And Marcel uses this perception time and again in the story.

Marcel's own complex character, also, cannot fail to make us think about Freud's ideas on human development. Marcel certainly fits loosely into Freud's category of the Oedipal man, deeply attached to his mother and finding it difficult to sustain relations with women. Proust himself would almost certainly have heard Freud mentioned in his father's and brother's medical circles, though a general awareness of Freud's work was slow to come in France. However, Proust acknowledged no influence from Freud, nor does he himself offer anything that could remotely be called a Freudian account of Marcel. Marcel obviously sees a similarity between his childhood feelings about his mother and his later feelings towards women; but he specifically denies any belief in a causal link between the one and the other. Moreover, neither Proust nor Marcel sees Marcel's condition as a neurotic one. On the contrary, Marcel is portrayed as being more in command of his experience, better equipped in the end to take human advantage of it, than practically anyone else in the book. There is no suggestion that if Marcel could go back to his childhood and understand his repressed desires, all would be easier and better for him. Marcel's sufferings and disappointments in adult life, bitter though they are, are what he needs for his appreciation of the human condition; and they help him to dominate that condition with an unusual degree of success. Marcel is no simple Freudian unfortunate.

The question remains, of course, whether a Freudian view of

Proust can be illuminating for us, even if it has very little in common with the tone and thrust of Proust's own intellectual challenge to us. After all, whether he knew it or not, Proust might have been depicting, in his study of Marcel, a classic case of 'unsuccessful transference', let us say – the failure of a son to direct feelings that are appropriately addressed to his mother when he is a child, to other women when he is an adult. Freudian critics of Proust have energetically followed up this line of thought. They have portrayed Marcel as being surrounded by every kind of unsatisfactory family-substitute: brother-substitutes not only in Saint-Loup, but also in Gilberte and Albertine, mother-substitutes in Oriane and Odette, father-substitutes in Swann and Charlus (and 'fathers-in-art' in Elstir and Bergotte). Moreover, these figures, which are all of course invented by Proust, are simultaneously regarded as being fantasy equivalents of similar substitutes in Proust's own life.

The trouble is, as one of Proust's Freudian critics, Randolph Splitter, has himself put it, that 'there is no solution to these dizzying vortices of identification, projection and displacement'. We might add that there is as little evidence for these inner processes in Proust's life – even in the degree to which it is possible to grasp the idea of them – as there inevitably is in the purely fictional life of Marcel. For Proust's subtle account of ambiguous human feeling we get a confused one; for his sparkling intelligibility, the substitute that we are offered is something unintelligible.

Freud himself was diffident about offering substitutes for the accounts of human life contained in works of literary genius. Some of his followers have been more ready to 'shatter the surface unity of discourse' in a great work, to use another of Splitter's phrases – to take the text of a work and force quite different conclusions out of it from those offered by the original author. One cannot *a priori* question such an undertaking; but it must be judged by its success. For Freudians, it is perfectly natural to want to understand Proust in their own terms. But no such accounts have yet superseded Proust's own story. *A la recherche* retains its intellectual pre-eminence over all subsequent attempts to say what happened to Marcel.

Proust's art

That is the story, then, of how Marcel, the chief character in *A la recherche*, comes to perceive his unique destiny, and to write his unique book. Through the medium of Marcel's thoughts on the question, it also gives a partial account of what kind of book it is. But, of course, *A la recherche* is not only Marcel's book; it is also Proust's. And Proust's art takes it a long way beyond even the bounds of Marcel's aesthetics.

We said in the first chapter that what makes Marcel's memories so interesting is not just the way he comes to remember them, but also the fact that he has so much to remember. But he himself does not provide most of what he remembers. That is provided by Proust. For Marcel, what other people do is just something that happens to him. In no way does he, as a character in the novel, *create* those other people. Proust creates them; that is the difference.

In fact, with just the same effect as the traditional novel, Proust invents a body of characters in whom we see reflected the ways of a society and the real people who constitute it. This is the point we have emphasised in the earlier chapters of this study on society and love in *A la recherche*. (It would exactly catch the way in which everything recurs with a new contextual force in *A la recherche*, if we repeated those chapters here.) In few great novels, in fact, do we find so many characters whose changing fate and self-revelations we follow with such excitement – follow, moreover, through so many years and such extraordinary vicissitudes. Swann, Charlus, Robert, Oriane, Rachel – these are figures whose intense and complicated histories of sexual and social destiny prove unforgettable to most readers of Proust. There is no lack of contact here with life as we have to live it. And there are hundreds of other characters, most of whom one cannot even mention in a short study like this, some of them appearing only once, but most of them recurring across the pages of the book, found there in new situations and offering further – often startling – insights into their nature.

Proust thrusts people into Marcel's path as abundantly as the people that crowd to meet the little train on the railway from Balbec to La Raspelière. We are led back to the fact that this is not really a memoir but a novel. Proust has set up a framework for Marcel that is outside Marcel's own aesthetic considerations and his artistic programme for himself. We must not be seduced by Marcel's passionate subjectivism into forgetting this fact. Earlier critics of Proust were too inclined to do this, to see *A la recherche* as little more than a disguised autobiography, in which the reverberations of Proust's sensitivity, and the aesthetic declarations and discoveries made by Marcel, were the exclusive point of interest.

Marcel's aesthetics cannot allow for this extra aspect of the book he is writing: he just takes as gifts of chance what are really Proust's gifts to him. Nevertheless, some of his remarks hint at it. He is, in effect, alluding to it when he talks in that affectionate but slightly disparaging way about the Muse of History, who seems, on Marcel's estimate, to be little more than the Muse of Gossip. It is quite appropriate for Marcel here, as a character obsessed with his own ideas about art, to play down what Proust is doing for him – namely, allowing the vast 'contingent' world of family and society to appear merely as a kind of outcrop of Marcel's self-discovery and self-conquest. However, we ourselves can see that this Muse is really someone much more important, as Proust well knows: no one less than the traditional Muse of Fiction.

In fact, of course, Proust was perfectly well-acquainted with her. By the time he wrote *A la recherche*, he had entirely absorbed the art of the great comic and realistic novelists both in France and England. Balzac's great panorama of French society in the seventeen volumes of *La comédie humaine* was an especial challenge to him. He was careful, in print, never to praise Balzac unreservedly. He was very insistent that he was trying to establish an art that went far beyond Balzac's. But there is a telling anecdote of him talking to a friend, Jacques Porel, the son of the actress Réjane, in 1917. 'He spoke so vividly of Balzac one evening when they dined together,' says George Painter, 'that Porel had the eerie impression that Balzac himself would soon enter the restaurant and sit at their table.' That same night he declared that Dickens's *Bleak House* was one of his favourite novels. Balzac, Flaubert, Dickens — George Eliot and Thomas Hardy, too — all played a part in bringing him to the idea of his own novel. They are precursors of 'Proust's art', in the sense we have been using it here, even more clearly than Baudelaire and Ruskin are precursors of 'Marcel's art'.

Morality and art

There is one aspect even of the traditional fictional side of *A la recherche* that has always troubled English readers: its morality. Though Proust acknowledged the interest to him of the nineteenth-century English novelists, the clear moral note that we associate with them, and appreciate in them, is not to be heard in Proust.

We might say that novels can make a moral appeal to us in three ways. They can present us with the moral strivings of a character, such as Dorothea in George Eliot's *Middlemarch*, and try to draw us into sympathetic feeling for the character's endeavours. They can portray acts of flagrant cruelty, in which we feel irresistible sympathy for the victim, and instant hatred of the perpetrator. Or, more subtly, they can lead us to align or identify ourselves first with one character, then another, and finally show us one of the two characters harming the other. In this way, because the character who causes the harm is already in some sense 'us', we are led into moral self-awareness and self-criticism, by a means that is peculiar to the novel, and that represents its supreme moral power.

But we can scarcely find any of these kinds of moral appeal in *A la recherche*. Among all the many characters of the novel, not one is steadily trying to achieve moral goodness, or to 'save his soul', in the way Dorothea is. On the contrary, such strivings are scrutinised in a very sceptical way even when they do, briefly, occur. Marcel is charmed by the excited socialist idealism of the young Saint-Loup, who has inherited all the advantages of being born into the aristocracy; but he sees the realism, in questions of power, of Saint-Loup's bigoted uncle, Charlus, as being far more likely to have tangible results, should Charlus ever be inclined to perform a 'good' action. Those men, like young

Saint-Loup, who 'obey an inner ideal' which drives them to rid themselves of their advantages resemble, for Marcel, 'the painters and writers who renounce their virtuosity, the warrior people who initiate universal disarmament', and for whom 'as often as not the sequel fails to reward their noble efforts; for the artists lose their talent, the nations their age-old predominance; pacifism often breeds wars and tolerance criminality' (I P757, K813).

Even simple moral states of mind like gratitude are called into question. We only feel real gratitude, Marcel thinks, towards a woman we love who shows us physical kindness; generally speaking, we are indifferent to the amiability of others. Repeatedly, in this way, Marcel portrays virtuous acts and attitudes as mere side-effects of people's hopes and fantasies about their relationships with other people.

And even what we might regard as the undeniable wickedness of certain acts is often softened and diffused by Marcel in a similar way. There is a moment when the young Marcel, exploring Paris, discovers that 'almost every house sheltered some unhappy person ... quite half of the human race was in tears' (II P372, K386). But as soon as he starts thinking about who is responsible for this state of affairs – the unfaithful wives, the drunken sons who beat their mothers – he begins to wonder what the deceived husbands and the beaten mothers have themselves done to bring it about. At times, indeed, he wonders whether anyone can really be said to be doing anything to anybody else at all. 'There are, after all, no individuals,' he remarks, meaning that none of us, whether villain or victim, clearly perceives another person: all that we do is a wholly subjective affair, a pursuit of the projections of our own mind, whether we imagine we are being kind and loving, or whether we are gratifying ourselves with the idea that we are hurting someone, or even whether we are imagining that other people are hurting us (II P908, K946).

Only occasionally does some outrage strike Marcel so deeply that he conveys a feeling of deep indignation to us; and these are usually acts of cruelty towards the exceptionally weak and powerless – towards servants, or elderly parents. One such instance is when the Duchesse de Guermantes deliberately makes a valet miserable, by keeping him in the house on a pure pretext when she knows he is longing to meet his fiancée. Another is when the daughter and son-in-law of the great actress, Berma, let themselves be lured to a party by her hated rival, Rachel – and even allow themselves to be publicly humiliated by her there – while Berma herself is on her death-bed. Yet even in these situations, the participants, whether they appear as the ones who inflict the suffering or the ones who suffer, seem to be locked in private preoccupations that sweep them on to inevitable clashes, with quite arbitrary and unpre-dictable consequences. So the shock of disgust that we feel eventually subsides. The same is very much the case with Charlus's insults to Mme de Saint-Euverte at the Princess's reception; or with the revenge that Mme Verdurin takes on Charlus for his humiliation of her, when she turns Morel's affections away from him.

So striving for virtue, striving to harm, and even harming are not seen to have the importance that morality usually attributes to them. On the other hand, Marcel does recognise the presence of a certain very simple kind of virtue among men. It is some-thing spontaneous, unconsidered – a kindness that 'blossoms of its own accord' – and at one stage in the story Marcel even remarks that this sort of kindness is 'the commonest thing in the world' (I P741, K796). He associates it with ancient French and Christian virtues, as pictured in the church porches at Combray and Balbec. For instance, in a bas-relief at Balbec, a husband, as he helps his young wife to rise from the grave on the Day of Judgement, holds her hand against his own heart to reassure her that it is beating. But later he speaks of finding this quality only in one place – in the family of Combray, his own family, including Françoise, who seem to take on the lineaments of the Holy Family itself as he writes about them here.

Even among his own family, though, only one person really illustrates the point. We get few glimpses of Marcel's own mother and father, and Françoise, when she appears, mainly provides examples of how this natural virtue can be 'paralysed', as Marcel is quick to tell us, 'by self-interest' (I P741, K796). The character who most consistently displays this unreflective sweetness is Marcel's grandmother. After she dies, we meet little human kindness in Marcel's world.

Yet his grandmother's gentleness coalesces with what is at first sight a very different feature of Marcel's personality. His grandmother, he says, 'enjoyed the diversity of other people without expecting anything of them or resenting anything that they did' (II P911, K941). Now this is also true of Marcel. But if, according to him, he had inherited this trait from his grandmother, to us it seems to derive just as clearly from his profoundly solipsistic beliefs. The pervasive solipsism in human conduct that we have already seen evoked as an explanation and an excuse for what might at first look like immorality encourages a tolerance in Marcel. He gives us one example of how this works in practice when he says that he is not inclined to condemn other people's cowardice, because when he is brave he knows it is not for a moral reason, but just to preserve his self-esteem. That is, after all, as egoistic a motive as other people's desire to save their skin. He feels that the one motive is no worse or better than the other – so why should he condemn the cowards?

This tolerance often shades into positive tenderness when Marcel contemplates other people closely. A good example is when, coming back to Paris in the middle of the 1914–18 war, he finds most wealthy Parisians heartlessly taking advantage of the material and social opportunities the war has given them, and in a general way is revolted by the fact. But while walking through the Paris night, turning these thoughts over, he suddenly sees the Baron de Charlus – and though it is easy to point to ways in which Charlus, too, has dissociated himself from the fighting and slaughter, a warmth towards this curious individual comes into Marcel's voice as he describes him, and his other thoughts are forgotten. It is the same when he is describing the general indifference towards the deaths at sea. He passes on to the story of how Mme Verdurin hears of the sinking of the *Lusitania*. She reads the news at breakfast; but it is the first morning for a long time that she has been able to get any of her favourite croissants. She is appalled by the news, but she is taking it in at just the moment when she is biting her first croissant, and the expression that crosses her face is a smile. It ought to make us squirm − but it does and it doesn't. For a delicate understanding of Mme Verdurin's very ordinary human frailty warms and quickens Marcel's account of the scene.

We can say, then, that sceptical though Proust shows himself to be about the sources of most moral endeavour and most moral judgements, he is not an enemy of morality. By putting conventional moral ideas through such scrupulous tests he is not doing them a disservice; and, above all that, his whole novel is on the side of generosity and forgiveness − indeed, of a ruefully realistic love of mankind.

There is one further moral idea in the book, perhaps the one that is most important of all to Proust. The endeavour to create a work of art is presented throughout as an unquestionably heroic undertaking. The suffering he undergoes in his love for Albertine is finally accepted by Marcel because of the understanding it gives him of himself, and the profound contribution that in turn makes to his book. 'There is not a woman in the world the possession of whom is as precious as that of the truths which she reveals to us by causing us to suffer,' he says after Albertine's death (III P496, K506). As their books are one and the same, I think we may take Marcel's view here to be Proust's also.

Furthermore, when the writer Bergotte dies, Proust speaks of the dedication of an artist to his work as though it were identical, in essence, with heroic moral endeavour. It is the only time in the book when he writes of the latter with such intensity of feeling, and its claims are plain enough:

All that we can say is that everything is arranged in this life as though we entered it carrying a burden of obligations contracted in a former life; there is no reason inherent in the conditions of life on this earth that can make us consider ourselves obliged to do good, to be kind and thoughtful, even to be polite, nor for an atheist artist to consider himself obliged to begin over again a score of times a piece of work the admiration aroused by which will matter little to his worm-eaten body, like the patch of yellow wall painted with so much skill and refinement by an artist destined to be forever unknown and barely identified under the name Vermeer. All these obligations, which have no sanction in our present life, seem to belong to a different world, a world based on kindness, scrupulousness, self-sacrifice, a world entirely different from this one and which we leave in order to be born on this earth, before perhaps returning there to live once again beneath the sway of those unknown laws which we obeyed because we bore their precepts in our hearts, not knowing whose hand had traced them there − those laws to which every profound work of the intellect brings us nearer. . .

They buried him, but all through that night of mourning, in the lighted shop-windows, his books, arranged three by three, kept vigil like angels with outspread wings and seemed, for him who was no more, the symbol of his resurrection. (III P187−8, K186)

Proust and Marcel

It is important to stress Proust's place in the family of traditional novelists. But our last point must be that Proust keeps faith with Marcel. Marcel's truths are, after all, part of Proust's truths, and 'Marcel's art' is in no way to be set against Proust's art. What we have called 'Proust's contribution' to Marcel's story is always wholly absorbed into that story, in which Marcel's presence is felt in every line.

There are two apparent contradictions to be resolved here. Marcel's account of other people stresses the impossibility of knowing other people − the point that is made above all through his extraordinary portrait-that-is-not-a-portrait of Albertine. How, then, can his portrayal of so many of the people around him have so much in common with that of traditional novels?

Again, it is often said that the characters in *A la recherche* all have something in common with Marcel; indeed we have frequently noticed the way in which the experience of other characters prefigures or echoes that of the narrator. Yet most readers feel that the variety and individuality of the other characters is one of the strongest impressions left on us by the novel. How can this be?

Our first answer lies in the subtle concession Marcel makes in the matter of knowing other people. He allows that by examining our own feelings we may sometimes deduce the feelings that are concealed in others. If that is so, and if Marcel is to be consistent about perceiving other people's feelings only through the medium of his own, it is not surprising that we shall find similarities between other characters and himself. Indeed, as part of the longed-for unity of his book, that fact will give him (as it gives us) great satisfaction.

However, the limitations seemingly implied by that are heavily qualified by one of the other main aspects of Marcel's character: namely, his complexity and instability. In fact, in Walt Whitman's phrase, he 'contains multitudes'. That may be his affliction, as a man who wants a sense of his own coherence; but as a perceiver of other people's natures through his own, it gives him an exceptional advantage − because he is able to find something in common between himself and so many *different* kinds of person. Being sexually, socially and temperamentally poised on so many frontiers, he is able to look in all directions and find other men and women mirrored in himself, and himself in them.

We must also not forget that he does not rule out observation as a human faculty. He sometimes remarks that he has a poor eye for detail, but that just seems a side-swipe at artists who practise a more limited, surface realism. 'Involuntary memory' and its related powers in fact bring back everything, in all its sensuous fullness and freshness, besides all its subjective associations. With these powers, in addition to his many-sided character, Marcel is in the end formidably equipped to present us with portraits of the people he meets, without in any way compromising his scepticism about mutual understanding between people. And that is what Proust allows him to do.

Finally, Marcel remains throughout the book a fully-created character. He makes a concession about self-knowledge that Proust also, so to speak, takes maximum advantage of. Just as we may sometimes understand other people's feelings through our own, Marcel says, so we may perceive our own behaviour more clearly by observing other people's. Marcel, as a character, is allowed in this way to learn certain elusive facts about himself, and so portray his behaviour in retrospect with a degree of detachment or irony. More than that, however, Proust delicately allows him at times to convict himself of absurdity without full consciousness of it — as in his great bow to the Duc de Guermantes. We are allowed to remember Legrandin's bow, and make our comparison, at that point — but Marcel, prodigious rememberer though he is, gives no sign of remembering it himself.

Let us come back from Marcel to Proust, writing his book in the Boulevard Haussman in the last years of his life. By 1914, he had completed a version of his novel. But only the first volume, *Du côté de chez Swann*, was published before the war; and during the war Proust revised and enormously extended the book. He went on doing this up to the last minute before the printing of each of the subsequent volumes that came out in his lifetime, from 1919 onwards. The pre-1914 book was about half a million words in length; the final *A la recherche* was one and a quarter million. At one time it was thought that this tremendous expansion of the novel from its pre-war version was coloured by an increasing misanthropy in the personality attributed to Marcel. But a recent, more thorough study by Alison Winton shows that Proust was completely faithful to his original conception of the novel during these years, enriching and deepening every facet of it equally.

Had he lived longer, he would undoubtedly have made further corrections — and additions, too, in all probability. In the later pages there are some contradictions that he would have undoubtedly cleared up. In particular, several characters are described as dead, and then appear again: they include Dr Cottard, one of the members of Mme Verdurin's clan, and the Marquise de Villeparisis, Marcel's first connection with the Faubourg.

But Proust seems to have died, on 18 November 1922, with the feeling that his work was essentially complete. Even those remaining contradictions in the story acquire a peculiar aptness in their context. Marcel himself observes, in *Le temps retrouvé*, that one of the dreadful signs of old age is that people forget whether their friends are alive or not. So we may think of Marcel, the narrator, as naturally forgetting such things himself; and of even this forgetfulness as finding a proper place in Proust's display of the contents of human memory.

For Proust gives us as remarkable an account as there exists in fiction of the life of a richly varied and complex society — and passes it off as one man's entirely personal experience. He unites a searching worldly realism and an exalted solipsistic romanticism in such a way that we cannot separate them out: each depends entirely on the other for its expression. That is why *A la recherche* is one of the greatest attempts ever made to record the experience of human life in its totality.

Note on the English translations

The Anglo-Saxon world quickly learned about Proust. Early in 1914, for example, Henry James, living in London, obtained a copy of *Du côté de chez Swann*, which had been published the previous November, and wrote to tell him that it was the greatest French novel since Stendhal's *La Chartreuse de Parme*.

The second volume of the book, *A l'ombre des jeunes filles en fleurs*, was set up in proof in 1913, but not published till 1919 because of the war. *Le côté de Guermantes* and *Sodome et Gomorrhe* were published in four volumes between 1920 and 1922. The last three volumes were published after Proust's death in November 1922: *La prisonnière* in 1923, *Albertine disparue* (subsequently renamed *La fugitive*) in 1925 and *Le temps retrouvé* in 1927.

C. K. Scott Moncrieff was at work on his English translation before Proust died, and his first volume, *Swann's Way*, appeared in September 1922. Scott Moncrieff went on with the task, and completed all except the last of the twelve volumes into which his translation was divided, before he died in 1930. Stephen Hudson (a pseudonym for Stephen Schiff) translated the last volume, *Time Regained*; it was later retranslated in the United States by Frederick Blossom, and in Britain by Andreas Mayor.

However, in 1954, a completely new edition of *A la recherche* was published in France in the *Bibliothèque de la Pléiade*. As we have seen, only one volume had been published before the First World War, and Proust went on continuously revising and expanding the manuscript of all the other volumes. He also altered the proofs of those volumes published between 1919 and 1922, up to the last possible minute. As a result, the whole of the first edition of *A la recherche*, except for the first volume, contained errors of decipherment and omissions. The *Pléiade* editors, working from the manuscripts and the proofs, tried to establish a version as close as possible to what seemed to be Proust's final intentions.

So in 1981 a new edition of Scott Moncrieff's translation, revised by Terence Kilmartin, was published. The intention was that the new version should correspond in most respects with the *Pléiade* edition. Kilmartin took the opportunity of correcting many errors made by Scott Moncrieff, and also, where appropriate, of amending the style of the translation where it diverged too greatly from Proust's original tone. Scott Moncrieff had a distinct liking for the florid phrase, the markedly poetical expression, and in this way he sometimes adds to Proust's precise poetry an extra aura of his own. Kilmartin would be the first to acknowledge the extent to which his version depends on the original labours of Scott Moncrieff; but he has certainly produced what is in the end a closer and better translation.

The passage about Andrée's hands quoted on page 60 provides a good example of the difference between the two versions. Where Kilmartin describes Andrée's hands as 'far more delicate', Scott Moncrieff has 'much finelier modelled', an elaboration that has no authority in Proust's '*bien plus fin*', and causes the sentence to pause too long over the point. Further on, Kilmartin's 'and used often to stretch out before her like thoroughbred greyhounds' replaces Scott Moncrieff's 'and used often to strain out before her like a leash of thoroughbred greyhounds'. The French is '*et elles s'allongeaient souvent devant elle comme de nobles lévriers*'. Scott Moncrieff has missed the point of '*s'allongeaient*' here, which means precisely to 'stretch out' like a dog in front of the fire (the fire which actually comes in, in Elstir's painting, a moment later); by translating it as 'strain out' he has had to invent a 'leash' of greyhounds that is not there in Proust. And the physical sensation of a dog stretching out which we noticed earlier in the rhythm of Kilmartin's sentence, echoing Proust, is lost, along with the meaning, in Scott Moncrieff's longer phrase. Scott Moncrieff does use the word 'stretchings' in the next line — 'stretchings of a joint' — which may be why he avoided it just before. But again Kilmartin has the more correct, which is also not surprisingly the more expressive, word — '*flexings* of a finger-joint' (in the French, *étirements d'une phalange*) which, as we have seen, unites the metaphor of the greyhound to the finger with perfect rightness. Incidentally, few exercises could demonstrate the sureness of Proust's language in *A la recherche* better than a comparison like this between the two English versions.

Further reading

Works by Proust in the original French

A la recherche du temps perdu, 3 vols. *Bibliothèque de la Pléiade*, Paris, 1954.

Contre Sainte-Beuve, with *Pastiches et mélanges* and *Essais et articles*. *Bibliothèque de la Pléiade*, Paris, 1971.

Jean Santeuil, with *Les plaisirs et les jours*. *Bibliothèque de la Pléiade*, Paris, 1971.

Works by Proust in translation

Remembrance of Things Past. Translated by C. K. Scott Moncrieff, revised by Terence Kilmartin. 3 vols, London and New York, 1981.

Jean Santeuil. Translated by Gerard Hopkins. London, 1955.

Pleasures and Days, and Other Writings. Edited by F. W. Dupee, translated by Louise Varese, Gerard Hopkins and Barbara Dupee. New York, 1957.

Marcel Proust on Art and Literature, 1896–1919 (containing *Contre Sainte-Beuve*). Translated by Sylvia Townsend Warner. New York, 1958.

Works on Proust in English or English translation

The standard life of Proust in English is the remarkable and pioneering *Marcel Proust* by George D. Painter (2 vols, London, 1959 and 1965). *Proust: Collected Essays on the Writer and his Art* by J. M. Cocking (London, 1982) and *Proust* by Roger Shattuck (London, 1974) are two excellent studies. Roger Shattuck's earlier book, *Proust's Binoculars* (London, 1964), develops its arguments from a consideration of Marcel's way of seeing. Leo Bersani's *Marcel Proust: The Fictions of Life and Art* (New York, 1965) is, above all, a searching study of Marcel. Malcolm Bowie's lecture, *Proust, Jealousy, Knowledge* (London, 1978) concentrates on *La prisonnière*, and the relationship in Marcel between sexual jealousy and the desire for knowledge. Alison Winton's *Proust's Additions: The Making of 'A la recherche du temps perdu'* (2 vols, Cambridge, 1977) is an illuminating study of the way the novel grew between 1913 and 1922. *Proustian Space* by Georges Poulet (translated from the French by Elliott Coleman, Baltimore, 1977) is full of insights developing out of the idea that divisions of space, rather than time, are what Marcel seeks to overcome. Gerard Genette's *Narrative Discourse* (translated from the French by Jane E. Lewin, Oxford, 1980) is a detailed and original study of narrative technique, taking its examples from Proust. Walter Benjamin's *Illuminations* (translated from the German by Harry Zohn, London, 1970) is a collection of essays of which two concern Proust, 'The Image of Proust' and 'On Some Motifs in Baudelaire'.

Index

The index is divided into two parts: I People and Places (and one newspaper); II Fictitious People and Places in *A la recherche*. Various themes are indexed under the headings 'Proust, Marcel', 'Albertine' and 'Marcel'.

II FICTITIOUS PEOPLE AND PLACES IN 'A LA RECHERCHE'

OXFORD

MORE PAST MASTERS

Details of a selection of other Past Masters follow. A complete list of Oxford Paperbacks, including The World's Classics, Twentieth-Century Classics, OPUS, Oxford Authors, Oxford Shakespeare, and Oxford Paperback Reference, is available from the General Publicity Department, Oxford University Press (JH), Walton Street, Oxford, OX2 6DP.

In the USA, complete lists are available from the Paperbacks Marketing Manager, Oxford University Press, 200 Madison Avenue, New York, NY 10016.

Oxford Paperbacks are available from all good bookshops. In case of difficulty, please order direct from Oxford University Press Bookshop, 116 High Street, Oxford, Freepost, OX1 4BR, enclosing full payment. Please add 10 per cent of published price for postage and packing.

MONTAIGNE

Peter Burke

Montaigne created a new literary genre—the essay—and his own essays have had a widespread influence on thought and literature since the Renaissance. In them he put forward ideas on a wide variety of subjects viewed as highly unconventional by his contemporaries, and because of this he has often been treated as a 'modern' born out of his time. Peter Burke replaces him in his cultural context, and shows what he had in common with his Renaissance contemporaries.

'this brisk and lively introduction . . . provides, in a tiny compass, a balanced view and a clear and eminently readable account of the issues Montaigne tried to grapple with' *British Book News*

'a handbook for students of unique wisdom and tolerance' *Tablet*

PETRARCH

Nicholas Mann

Steeped in the medieval culture which had produced Dante, yet in his passionate interest in classical antiquity one of the founding fathers of the Renaissance, Petrarch has a real claim to be considered the first modern man. This study (the only brief introduction to Petrarch available in English) explores that modernity through a series of often conflicting but always interlocking images of himself which Petrarch projects in his writings: the traveller and intellectual deeply interested in the writings of antiquity; the man of action and contemplation; and the poet laureate and moralist.

'a remarkable book' *Modern Language Review*